Merchant Navy -
Heroes and Half-Wits

By Bob Jackman

This edition published in Great Britain in 2011
by
Farthings Publishing
SCARBOROUGH
YO11 2QB
UK

Copies available from the author
Bob Jackman
12 Highdale Road
SCARBOROUGH
YO12 6LL
Tel: 01723 365396

Or online through
http://www.Farthings-Publishing.com

ISBN 978-1-4466-1718-2

March 2011 (b)

CONTENTS

PREVIOUS BOOKS BY BOB JACKMAN

SHARK
Diverse Verses

PREFACE

B eing at anchor or alongside in remote corners of the world drove me to write memoirs of my life as a Merchant Navy engineer.

I now write them when they come to mind, stories about great lads I had sailed with, bum companies I had sailed in, daft things that had happened and nothing is in any chronological order. I sailed with all nationalities on anything that floated, from tugs to tankers, cargo ships to coasters for forty-one sweet years.

Most of all, I have written about the fellows I have sailed with, and irrespective of whether they be 'goodies' or `baddies', to me, they are a breed of men that stand high above all others.

I published 'SHARK' in 2004 and it is still selling well. In this book, I sing the praises of many great guys I had the pleasure to sail with. Others should contact lawyers.

This is a collection of stories about the men I sailed with during my forty-one years at sea, forty-one years that began in 1950. Many started from a humble back ground, others from wealthy parentage and there were some who began life in the Homes for Misplaced Children. They became united members of the family of officers and men on board ship and each had stories to tell.

This always leads to an amazing assortment of tales

about other ships, other companies, other corners of the world and other fellow officers they had sailed with.

All Merchant Navy Officers have great stories to tell. These are some of mine.

INTRODUCTION

So many stories are told about sailors, ships and amazing voyages travelled by noble Captains. I know many of those Captains I have sailed with laugh at the tales presented to the public; Captains like Lorrimer, Bazill, Hooper, Greatorex, Sladovitch, Smythe, and other great men too numerous to mention.

This book, Merchant Navy : Heroes and Half-wits, is about the real men of the British Merchant Navy.

In my forty years I sailed with those men in Nourse Line, City Line, Williamson's Hong Kong, Elder Dempster's, Mullion's Hong Kong, and Scottish Ship Management until high blood pressure ruled me out of my world of deep sea shipping.

The only life left for me was the coastal trade and I had more than a few laughs there with the lads on coasters. In fact I sailed in anything that could move and stay afloat at the same time.

I'm 81 years old now and I miss all those wonderful lads I sailed with, in those forty years.

God bless them. No one else does.

Bob Jackman
2011

SUNBURNT

It all happened in Karachi in 1950. In those days we could be in port for two or even three weeks and nearly every ship we saw was flying the 'Red Duster'.

As Fourth Engineer the responsibility of maintaining the lifeboat engine fell upon my broad shoulders every time we had a Saturday boat drill. Consequently I checked and serviced that little Morris Vedette engine regularly.

It was during breakfast on a Sunday when Paul, our redheaded Second Mate, suggested putting the lifeboat down in the water and giving her a run.

'What do you say, Bob? We take our deck cadets along and give them a bit of boating experience. It'll be good for them and we'll be back in time for lunch.'

So Paul, the three young deck cadets and I lowered the lifeboat into the water and scrambled down the Jacob's ladder. She was an old ship and lowering lifeboats was an awkward task that required a degree of skill. Lifting the lifeboat was an even more difficult task that required the use of a couple of main cargo winches and some of the crew.

So we merrily sailed down the main channel with ships of all kinds on either side. The lifeboat engine was throbbing away happily. Eventually the channel opened out into a large bay of sorts, with very distant shores.

'Hey, Bob, I suggest we stop the engine here and let our three whizz kids put up the mast and rig the sails. OK?' He turned to the cadets and barked. 'Right, you lot, look sharp.'

They cheerfully scurried about with the essentials while Paul and I watched without comment. But a lot of time passed before the sails were up. There was a gentle breeze, the sails filled but the lifeboat remained where she was. After a couple of minutes I picked up an oar to ascertain the depth beneath us and found we were aground in less than twelve inches of water.

It was 09.30 hours and the sun was already a bit too hot.

Paul jumped over the side with the boat's anchor and waded astern until he was up to his waist in the water, then dropped the anchor. Once he was sure it had some grip on the sandy bottom he returned to the lifeboat.

'Well, Bob, we can but try. Let's have a go!'

I started the engine, put her briefly into astern and all five of us hauled on the anchor rope. Nothing happened, our boat didn't budge one millimetre and I switched off the engine.

We sat down and surveyed the situation. The sun was climbing ever higher and becoming more uncomfortable. The cadets and I were all right but Paul's pale complexion and freckles were not suitable in this climate and his skin was turning quite red.

'Paul? I suggest you stay in the shade. Keep the sail between you and the sun.'

He looked at me and nodded.

'We'll need to find something to tow us off,' he murmured, his eyes scanning the horizon.

The only thing to be seen in that great expanse of water was an elderly native figure in a dug out canoe, so we bawled our heads off and he turned his craft towards us. It was literally a crude hollowed-out log and its owner's raiment consisted of two pieces of rag, one round his head, one round his hips.

I jabbered at him in my home-made Hindustani and we came to an agreement.

'What's happening, Bob?'

'Two things, Paul. There's a ferry of sorts somewhere over in that direction and he'll take me there. Secondly, I promised him twenty rupees'.

'Twenty rupees? That's not much.'

'Paul, dear friend, for twenty rupees this man would take all of us to the planet Jupiter and back. So, you, back in the shade and I'll go find us a ferry.'

I climbed in behind the dinghy wallah and we set off. It was a long way and we were very low in the water with about two inches of freeboard. He did a lot of paddling and I did a lot of baling. It seemed a long time passed before a jetty came into view and alongside the jetty lay a little ferryboat. It was little more than an old ship's lifeboat with an upper deck under a canvas awning.

Its twenty-odd passengers gaped at us as we approached and within minutes the ferryman and his assistant had his irate passengers stranded on the jetty with me on board his boat.

'You speak fifty rupees, sahib?'

'I speak fifty rupees good price.'

We set off the way I had just come with the intention of towing our lifeboat into deeper water but when we arrived, our lifeboat was marooned high and dry with not a lick of water anywhere near it. She looked positively incongruous stuck dead centre in a sandy island with her sails up.

I walked over and joined the others. Paul's skin was now a fiery red and peeling but the cadets were not too bad.

'Look, Paul, you take this ferry back to the ship and I'll stay here with the cadets. We'll sail it back to the ship. Or maybe the ferry could bring back the Mate or the Third Mate.'

He knew he was in a mess but wouldn't give up.

'I brought the lifeboat out, Bob, I'll take it back in. Remember, I'm responsible for it.'

'Stubborn twit,' I muttered under my breath, and then added. 'Okay, I'll take the ferry back to the ship and bring back some beers.'

So the ferry took me the long journey back to where we were berthed and I clambered up the rope ladder on to the deck. The Chief Engineer, Captain and the Mate were waiting on deck, sensing something was wrong and I rapidly relayed the whole story to them. Within minutes, Harry the Mate, was making up a box of burn dressings, petroleum jelly and a large straw hat. Our Indian Chief Steward produced a case of canned beers and a pair of white bed sheets. I went to my cabin and took a bundle of rupees from my desk to supplement those in my pocket.

The other officer on deck was the useless twit of a Third Mate. He fluttered around me trying to keep his face inches from mine and offered no assistance but wanted to know everything that had happened. He continued to stand directly in front of me, plying me with loads of stupid questions when I'm trying to get organised with loading the essentials into the ferry. He was an obstruction to me and everyone else and he would not listen to those telling him he was a damned nuisance.

Finally I was on the ferry and on my way back to the others to find that the size of our island had decreased considerably. I paid a delighted ferryman sixty rupees and immediately turned my attention to Paul. I found that his skin was blistering badly and the skin on his shoulders and his knees was now peeling off in patches as big as beer bottle labels.

'Right, Paul, Captain's orders, you take the ferry back to the ship and the cadets and I will follow when the tide comes in.'

He smiled at me. 'Good try, Bob, but it doesn't work. I took her out, I take her back.'

He was just one of those types of bloke.

It took more than a few minutes to get his shirt off and the mess his back and shoulders were in unnerved us a little. The petroleum jelly was generously smeared over all the burnt patches on his body then we applied the burn dressings. His shirt and two cotton bed sheets were used to cover him. He looked more like an Arab sheik than a Merchant Navy deck officer.

The beers were lovely and wet and we each had two. Our eyes kept straying to watch the water creeping closer to the boat.

'We do nothing until we feel the boat move,' Paul demanded. 'When she floats we'll pull her off, but not until then.'

'Okay by me,' I smiled to reduce the tension of the cadets. 'It would be a shame taking beers back.'

I had to keep cheery for their sake. It was nearly five in the afternoon and it was wearing them down a little. Some of the heat had gone out of the sun but we were all a bit red-raw and uncomfortable with it.

Our youngest cadet, Dean, took to sounding the depth of water with the boat hook and informing us of his findings. At fifteen inches we felt her move a little and we all smiled at each other.

'Take down the sails, lads.' Paul's voice was quite weak. 'And, dammit, make sure you stow them properly.'

After eight hours of doing nothing but sit under a blazing sun the young lads sprang into life. Sails and mast were quickly dismantled and stowed in good order then the three cadets looked at Paul for comments.

He smiled. 'Well, there's hope for you yet. Let's see if she'll move. Pull on the rope but don't pull too hard. Take her gently.'

So the cadets pulled on the anchor rope but though the boat rocked a little she wasn't ready to move out. We kept some tension on it then suddenly, minutes later, she eased herself out into the deeper water. We cheered and it seemed that the boat rocked a little, as if pleased to be free again. I started the engine and we headed for the main channel and back to the ship. Everybody wore a big smile now that the ordeal was over.

The sun that had caused us so much trouble was now sinking on the horizon and a light breeze sprang up. It almost felt cold.

Suddenly the engine was overheating.

It was now dusk, we were in the main shipping channel without lights and the old Morris Vedette engine had a cooling water problem. The cooling water supply came straight from the bottom of the boat to the cooling pump. No shut-off valve, no strainer, nothing! It had to be something clogging the suction pipe underneath the boat.

Now James Bond was a Scot. I'm a Scot, too, but there all similarity ends. There was no way I was going over the side of any boat in a main shipping channel at dusk in any of the waterways within a thousand miles of Karachi.

I cut the engine speed right down until it was lamely chugging along. We were making very slow progress against the incoming tide. If we stopped, we'd be carried back into the bay again so I kept her just ticking over.

Now it was quite dark and our ship was in sight, four ship lengths away. Finally, what seemed to be hours later, we arrived.

The cadets grabbed the pulley blocks and I stopped the engine. I could have thrown my arms around it and kissed it if I hadn't been so shattered.

I looked at the face with its fiery peeling skin and whispered. 'Paul? Can you climb the rope ladder? Are you fit enough?'

The Mate bawled down at us from the main deck. 'Bob. Put this rope round him gently, just in case.'

Paul stepped on to the rope ladder and muttered. 'Damn the rope!' He made his way slowly and painfully all the way up where eager hands helped him over the rail.

Meanwhile, in the lifeboat, our three cadets were struggling with the big pulley blocks that hook on to the lifeboat for lifting her back up on to the davits. With the swell, the lifeboat was bouncing up and down and trying to keep the blocks hooked to a lifeboat in these conditions had cost many a seaman his fingers.

'Take up the slack, up there!' I bawled with all the power my lungs could muster, but there was no reply. Some of the Indian crew looked over the ship's rail but didn't know what to do without orders from an officer on deck.

If those pulley blocks cost any of the cadets their fingers there'd be Hell to pay. I raced up the rope ladder, grabbed two of the Indian crew and took up all the slack in the ropes. The rest of the Indian crew whipped into action and rapidly wound the rope ends round the winch barrels. We lifted the lifeboat clear out of the water and left it dangling.

The Third Mate came out on deck as the cadets climbed on board. The Captain and the Chief Engineer appeared on the next deck up observing all that went on.

The Third Mate rushed at me, spluttering. 'You shouldn't have touched the ropes or the davits. That was my job! The Mate told me I was to do it. You had no right to do it!'

He was livid and his spluttering face was inches from mine. I was tired, my bones ached and I was in no mood to talk to the idiot.

'And where were you?' I asked politely.

'Seeing the Second Mate,' he stormed, almost jumping up and down in rage.

'The Captain, the Chief and the Mate were attending to the Second Mate. Why were you there as well?'

He screamed. 'BECAUSE I WANTED TO ASK HIM THINGS!'

In America it's called a 'Haymaker'. It seems when all the adrenalin in one's body is discharged into the muscles it momentarily provides an almost superhuman power. My clenched fist began its journey from somewhere behind my left ankle, travelled with the speed of light, connected with his jaw with all the power of a runaway locomotive and caused the Third Mate to land spread-eagled on the deck ten feet away.

'Okay, Bosun, bring her up.'

The lifeboat was raised and fitted into the davits. Then the Serang told his men to tidy up the ropes and 'knock off'. He looked at the spread-eagled Third Mate and whispered to me, 'You do good job, Sahib.'

I told the cadets to get washed and see if the Chief Steward had left out anything for their dinner.

The Third Mate was now sitting up, dazed, supporting himself against the hatch coaming. Suddenly he looked up at the Captain and the Chief and screamed. 'That Fourth Engineer hit me. He HIT me!'

They looked at each other. 'Did you see the Fourth Engineer hit the Third Mate, Chief?'

'No, Captain, I never saw the Fourth Engineer hit him. I think he must have fallen over something.'

They turned and went into the accommodation. The Third Mate still sat on the deck and whimpered, ignored by everyone.

I didn't care, I was tired, I went to my cabin, I had a beer and showered. End of story.

TWO MEN AND A MISSION

Al and I were buddies, but where I could enjoy a beer, he would have lemonade and where I liked night clubs, pubs and dancing girls his preference would be Seamen's Missions, movies and icecream. We were so different in our tastes, but good buddies nevertheless.

He was very much a 'tweed suit and pipe' sort of fellow who never had much to say, but girls were always attracted to him.

Generally, the Missions to Seaman in the world's ports are a popular place for seafarers, a place where they can meet respectable young ladies on dance nights and fellow seafarers from other ships on other nights.

Wonderful nights in Hong Kong, Adelaide, Capetown, Philadelphia and New York spring readily to mind.

Hong Kong, where the little padre / priest / minister would stick his head round the cabin door when we, the Engineer Officers, were having a cooling off beer after being on 'Stand By'. He would have a beer with us (honestly!) and consequently we always found time to have at least one night at his mission. He could laugh with us, tell a good story and yet give the impression that he'd been squaring things up with the Almighty just before we came into port.

At the Hong Kong Mission dances, Al soon had female admirers.

Again, in Port Adelaide, Australia the girls were tanned, wore cotton dresses, laughed easily and loved to take lads home for dinner and meet the family. Al turned down many dinner invitations and the others on board ship were seldom invited.

In Capetown, the Mission was actually a private club where Merchant Navy Officers were always welcome. There, a beautiful young lady in a wheelchair sat at piano and played requests. Five of us, rapidly fell madly in love with her and I swear she loved us a lot too, but Al most of all. When she spoke to him, her eyes said more than her mouth. And the guy wasn't even good-looking!

In Philadelphia, the Mission came under the title of 'The Ladies Auxiliary' and fell under the management of two rather elderly spinsters. Alcohol was taboo but we were generously served with crackers smothered in peanut butter and strawberry jam. This was accompanied with a teabag in a cup of hot water, no sugar, no milk. The evening drew to a close at ten o'clock when the girls left and the boys were not allowed to leave until quarter past. The usual routine was to meet the girls outside at the corner of 23rd and Beaver when the Mission closed then sallied into the Five-Five-Five Club, sometimes called The Little Bit Scotland. The musical 'Brig o' Doon' was all the rage in those far off days and since three of our group of four were Scots, we were made very welcome.

When we were being served at our table the waitress stopped her jaws working on her chewing gum long enough to ask if any of us were Scots.

I smiled sweetly and replied in the affirmative.

'Yeah? So let's hear you say 'murder', good and loud'

'Aye, lassie, I can say 'murder' but my English is no' awfy guid an' I dinna talk much American.'

'Hell, man, you sure is Scotch. So is the boss. Waal, all the drinks at this table are on the house.'

Officially, the bar closed at midnight but when two policemen arrived to check that local licensing laws were being strictly maintained they just happened to remember their grandmothers were Scots. Al spoke about the finer points of Scottish history and everybody hung on to every word he said. This presented some difficulties because, by this time, the waitress's face was three inches from his and she was nearly sitting on his lap.

As a result, the bar didn't close until three in the morning.

Another particular favourite of mine was the Seaman's Mission in New York, situated on the fifth floor in the Hotel Astor on Broadway. I remember four of us coming face-to-face with the lovely Greer Garson and having a few words with her in the entrance hall. On leaving us, she turned and waved to us, but her smiles were for Al.

Yes, most Missions were very popular with seafarers, but not all.

We had sailed from Antwerp in Belgium to Dublin in Ireland and where I suggested the effervescent Red Rooster night club in O'Connell Street and a few gallons of local beer, Al suggested a quiet evening at the Seamen's Mission, wherever it may be.

Again, why do I relent so easily? Why me? We went to the Seaman's Mission in Dublin.

The taxi took us on a long journey through the heart of Dublin down a myriad of narrow streets in an industrial area, lined on both sides with a grand array of derelict garages, scrapped cars and warehouses. The streetlights were on, a few stars peaked through the clouds and it was starting to rain. A lit sign above the entrance said 'ion' and closer inspection revealed the missing 'Miss' that should have preceded it.

We entered and found ourselves in a large hall with cracked paint on the walls and sheet wood covering broken windowpanes. In the dim light we observed a perimeter of assorted chairs where approximately seventeen assorted females sat chewing gum, smoking and chattering. The chattering dropped to a deathly silence when we appeared and seventeen haggard faces turned to look at us.

'Grab your horror for the Belsen tango,' I murmured. 'Al, let us get out and go back to all parts civilised. Pronto.'

I accept that not very woman can be a raving beauty and I can spread my affections quite cheerfully around those that are not, but not seventeen with daughters that must be years past their sell-by date when I was still in my very early twenties.

The sound of a gramophone gradually gathered speed as Al and I did an about turn to leave but we were ambushed by all sixteen of them. The only one who had not scrambled over to us had two walking sticks, smoked a pipe and was in charge of the gramophone.

One woman stood hard-pressed against me, her elbows holding off four others and her nose an inch from mine. 'We find boys who come here are too shy to ask for a dance so it's a Mission rule that the ladies ask the men.'

So Al and I were obliged to dance with two of them while their compatriots drooled, ogled us and sat quivering in anticipation. When the music stopped, we tried to back off but two others immediately grabbed us and the same record was played again. But it was Al they preferred.

We were better prepared when the music stopped for the second time and I almost made it to the pavement outside before my first dance partner caught up with me.

'Did you not just forget your prize, now? Here take it,' and she thrust a brown paper package into my hands.

'Thank you, thank you very much,' I gasped, still running backwards to keep her at an arm's length or a few yards more. She was trying to plant a big wet kiss on my face but I was resisting most powerfully.

'It's because, you were just the best dancer this week,' she panted, trying to pin me against a wall.

I prised her hands off my jacket lapels, pushed my knee hard against her stomach and broke free. I was probably her only dance partner in many weeks. Or months?

Al was staying a safe fifty yards ahead of me and ready to increase it further should any of the other ladies start to chase him.

We returned to the ship by taxi and joined the others in the officers' smoke room. I opened my prize and laid it on the bar. It was a large jar of home made useless marmalade.

We unfolded the evening's events to our fellow officers.

I ended with, 'and that was another time he ended up with women gazing up at him, completely enraptured.'

Al sighed, carefully laid his lemonade on the bar beside my beer and placed a hand on my shoulder. 'Well, Bob, think of it this way. You came to Ireland, met a crowd of ladies that threw themselves at you and in the end, you walked off with one of Dublin's top prizes for ballroom dancing.'

'Al, you twit, we've been to Hong Kong, Adelaide, Capetown, Philadelphia, New York and Dublin, and everywhere we go, girls are gazing deep into your eyes and you just laugh at them.'

He took a sip of his lemonade, and then smiled. 'They are fascinated, Bob, and do you know why? Because one of my eyes is blue, and the other eye is brown.'

And they were: One blue, one brown. Well, it's not the kind of thing fellows would notice, is it? But the girls did.

JAKE

The year was 1950. The 'Marjata' was my first ship, I was the highly inexperienced Fifth Engineer, and Jake was the Fourth Engineer.

Jake was tall, lean and bad. In company, he would patiently wait until someone would pass an innocent remark or crack a joke, and then he would take offence and try to provoke that inoffensive soul into a punch-up. But the evil Jake always chose to fight those who were no physical match for him.

There were occasions when he was known to lash out and hit a complete stranger passing in a quiet street for no reason other than it pleased him.

I remember one fight of sorts that Jake lost badly.

We'd had a month in Liverpool, six weeks round India, a long haul at nine knots round the Cape of Good Hope and up to Cuba.

Our cargo was bales of gunny bags for dozens of ports round the Caribbean. Some small ports received as little as a mere twenty bales and discharging in two ports in one day was not uncommon.

In the 1950s, all business matters in the small ports were conducted in the bars and the bars were conveniently situated on the dockside. When a ship came alongside, obliging customers would pop out, tie the ship up fore and aft and smartly return to the bar.

Within minutes, most of our European officers followed, leaving a few behind on duty.

To me, Cuba was a world where everyone laughed, played guitars, sang, shouted 'o-lay' and drank rum all day. There were fights, often with knives, but you didn't have to get involved if you didn't want to. There were girls, but, like the fights, you didn't have to get involved if you didn't want to.

Should customers become too boisterous, the armed police would come in, fire a few random shots and the bar would return to a respectable uproar.

In such ports, Jake tended to select his opponents with a modicum of care.

I remembered we anchored off San Pedro de Macoris to take on fuel from a small coastal oil tanker, a job that usually required two competent engineers. The senior of the two would 'take soundings' from the main deck as the tanks were filling. The other, the junior of the two, would be involved in running along the main deck, into the accommodation, down five flights of ladders to the bottom of the engine room, opening and closing the valves as required and dashing all the way up to the main deck again for further instructions.

An oil spill involved fines of many thousands of pounds and threw government officials at home and abroad into tantrums for ages.

But that particular day, the Chief told the Second. 'Leave it to the Fourth and the Fiver. They'll be OK.'

That was a classic remark from a man who had little idea of the capabilities of his engine room staff after being more than three months sailing with us. He never had the remotest idea what was happening 'down below' but as long as the engines performed well and the figures in the logbook pleased him, he was satisfied. He didn't want to know more, but he was still the Chief Engineer Officer and he felt it necessary to give a few orders occasionally.

Consequently, all hands were in the launch heading for the dockside bars when the little oil tanker chugged alongside us. Everyone that is, except Jake, the Third Mate and me. The tanker's bridge was level with our main deck and its Captain handed Jake a heaving line to pull the mooring line on board.

There was no sign of the Third Mate or any of the Indian crew but then, there never was when engineers were taking bunkers.

'Please, Senor?'

Jake stared at him blankly.

The little Captain stared back at him then stepped over the tanker's bridge rail with the rope. He was now moving sideways between the two ships and Jake was deliberately blocking his way, preventing him from climbing over the rail to board our ship. His crew of two young boys watched in horror from their main deck.

'Please, Senor!' The little man's voice was tinged with fear. If he was caught between the two ships as they nudged each other his whole body would be crushed flat and spread out like a large patch of strawberry jam.

Jake held his clenched fist under the old man's nose and brought his face down close.

'Who do you think you're pushing, you old bastard?'

I stepped between them and the old Captain hesitated for a moment, then clambered over the rail, pulled his mooring rope on board and over the nearest bollard. I stayed there, blocking Jake's path, daring him to push me aside while the old fellow and his two boys tied up the for'ard end and fitted their hose to the filling pipe.

Finally, Jake's finger poked me in the chest, but I could see he was undecided.

'You want to make trouble, Fiver?'

I knocked his hand away and smiled up at him.

'Yes, Jake. I'd like to make trouble. You want some?'

I knew he was wondering if he could beat me in a fight and I wasn't going to tell him he could. But like all bullies, he had a fear of being hurt and he backed down. He liked to be sure of his victories. His eyes looked past me to the tanker.

'Ah! The little Captain has family on board.'

I stepped away in case this was a ploy to wallop me, then turned to see a young girl on the bridge of the tanker watching us.

Keeping his eyes fixed on her, Jake murmured, 'I want you to go down the engine room and open the valves to number three port and starboard fuel tanks. Then come back and tell me when you've done it.'

The old Captain and his two boys were now safely on board their tanker. She was standing on the wing of the bridge, acting coy and girlish, allowing the warm breeze to blow her cotton dress against her slender figure.

I hurried all the way down to the bottom of the engine room, and opened the master filling valve and the two tank valves as Jake ordered. After a lightening check over main engine pressure and temperatures I rushed all the way up to the main deck and Jake.

'Right, Jake, number three port and starboard tank valves open, main filling valve on the for'ard bulkhead open and main engine temperatures and pressures are OK.'

My mad dash to the bottom of the engine room and back had knocked the breath out of me and he wasn't even listening. It was five decks down from the main deck to the bottom of the engine room and I had dashed down there and back.

His eyes were undressing the girl and she was loving it.

'Imagine that scrawny little rat having a gorgeous daughter like her,' he murmured.

'Right, Jake, shall we get on with the bunkering?' I was feeling far from confident in Jake's ability to take the fuel on board and I, a first tripper, knew I couldn't do it on my own.

'Yeah, sure. Tell them to start pumping. The sounding tape is on number three hatch. Let me know when the levels come up to three foot six inches.'

'You want ME to take the soundings? ME?'

'You'll be OK. I'll keep an eye on you.'

I trudged up the deck and waved to the oil tanker's Captain to start pumping the fuel on board. My heart was pounding louder than the tanker's old oil pump. I walked to the ship's rail to see if Jake was still within hailing distance in case I needed him and found he was not on deck anywhere.

The oil was coming in very fast and tank levels were coming up too quickly for comfort. I'd never taken fuel on board in my life. I'd never even *assisted* in taking fuel on board in my life. I had terrifying visions of oil gushing skywards all over the Caribbean and me not able to stop it.

I slid down the engine room ladders on handrails only, like an Olympic skier going for gold and cracked open the inlet valves to number two tanks. Number threes had been coming up too fast but opening number twos helped to slow things a little. Between ski-ing down and shooting up engine room ladders, taking soundings, switching tanks and opening and closing valves I was rapidly becoming a candidate for the nearest looney bin.

Two hours later came the sweetest words I ever heard on board any ship. 'Bunkering is finished, Senor.'

Both number two and three tanks were full and number fives were almost full. I had been up and down the engine room ladders about fifty times in two hours and I couldn't have done fifty-one. I slumped down on to the sun drenched deck and lay without moving.

The Captain and his two boys jumped on board and stepped over me to disconnect the filling pipe and let go the ropes.

Jake and the girl came out of the accommodation and made their way to the ship's rail. He swept her into his arms, gave her a long passionate kiss while we looked on, and then helped her over the rail, on to the bridge of the tanker. She giggled and blew him kisses before disappearing into the little tanker's accommodation.

Sweat was making my boiler suit stick to me, every muscle seem to have solidified and my bones ached, yet I managed to force my weary body up into a sitting position.

The tanker's engine started, throwing up clouds of thick black smoke and began to move away. The gap between the two ships widened and they were about ten feet apart when Jake shouted.

'Hey, Captain, I liked your daughter. She's hot stuff in bed!'

The gap between us was increasing slowly. The two crew boys stopped laying out the mooring ropes on the tanker's deck, looked at each other and burst out laughing.

'Did you hear me, you Spanish pig?' Jake screamed. 'I screwed your daughter twice. Twice! And she loved it!'

The Captain looked at Jake, waved pleasantly and smiled.

Jake's temper hit the record books. 'What are you pigs laughing at, eh?'

'Senor, forgive me, but she is not my daughter.'

Jake's temper cooled a little as his curiosity took over. 'She's not your daughter?'

'No, Senor.' The gap between the two ships had increased to twenty feet and the tanker was moving further away. 'She's a prostitute from Grilo Island. We take her to hospital in Havana.'

Jake clambered over me to keep up with the moving tanker. 'Hospital? Why is she going to hospital? What's wrong with her? Is she sick or something?'

'Maybe I should have told you before, Senor,' said the little Captain with a sad smile. 'She has syphilis very, very bad. They say maybe she have gonorrhoea, too, I think.'

Jake stood silently stunned on our main deck next to the sounding tape and the oily rags I'd been using, watching the tanker moving away. The little Captain and his two crew boys were now jumping up and down, waving at him and laughing.

I struggled to my feet and leaned against the bulwark then I started to laugh too. Yes, how I laughed.

Jake had just lost a battle!

Bob Jackman

STRANGE CHASTITY

It all began in a restaurant in the Japanese port of Yokkaichi when four of us tried to give an order of steak, egg and chips to a waiter who couldn't speak a word of English. Our assorted hand signals seemed to confuse the poor fellow and even Sparky's attempt at drawing steak, egg and chips on the back of the menu increased the problem. The Japanese diners were terribly amused and they secretly observed our predicament but no one could offer any assistance.

Until she spoke.

'Please? Perhaps I give you help?'

The offer came from a young Japanese lady sitting alone at a nearby table behind some potted palms. She was a beautiful creature who blushed slightly at her own temerity.

I jumped to my feet, startling the bewildered waiter while the others sat and gawped at her.

'You are very kind, miss, and as you can see we do need some help. We are harmless, hungry and strangers in your beautiful country.'

Her smile widened a few millimetres more and she lowered her eyes.

'Please, you speak what you like and I speak waiter.'

'All four of us would like steak, egg and chipped potatoes. We would also like you to sit with us at our table. Please?'

She hesitated, spoke to the waiter for a minute and looked up at me as if undecided. I knew she was considering whether or not it would be proper to be seen associating with four foreign seafarers. But we were quite smartly dressed and, in the eyes of the other diners, apparently well behaved.

To help persuade her, I whispered. 'You will be able to practice your English.'

The decision made, she rose from her table and came to ours. The other diners in the restaurant nodded and smiled their approval at her decision.

'This is very much wrong of me, but is good opportunity for speak my English.'

My three shipboard acquaintances were well off balance in the company of this lovely young lady. They coughed, looked askance at each other and were completely at a loss for words.

'My name is Bob. This is Sparky, Ossie and Gerry.'

She smiled and bowed her head to each in turn.

'My name is Horoko. Your food may take long time. When it comes, I will go. OK?'

'Bob is Scottish.' Sparky, who hailed from dear old Ireland, felt he had to say something. He was desperate to be included.

'Bob? Is Scottish language big different from English language?'

Her voice was soft, almost musical and I was having problems with my breathing when she looked at me. Heaven knows where my blood pressure was going.

'It's the same language but spoken differently. We are a very different people and different customs. Just different but same language.' I was in my late twenties and stammering like a schoolboy.

'I'm Sean. I'm from Ireland.' Sparky, the eldest of our noble band, wanted to play a leading roll in this romantic interlude but she was paying little attention to him. Our two remaining compatriots were beginning to lose their shyness.

'This is my first time in Japan,' Ossie mumbled. 'Been to India a lot. Well, twice.'

Little Gerry O'Hare, the youngest of our group, decided it was his turn to make a contribution to the conversation.

'I'm enjoying this. It's my first time in Japan. It's my first time anywhere! When I get home I'll tell the wife about being in Japan, talking with a Japanese lady and drinking Japanese beer.' His face was bright with excitement. He looked at each of us and explained. 'My Betty gets very angry if she hears I've been drinking.'

Horoko's face clouded. 'You are married to this wife?'

Gerry smiled, her phraseology amusing him. 'Yes, I am married to this wife.'

'In church with bible?'

'Yes, in church with bible.'

Horoko looked at him perplexed as she gave the matter some thought.

'She is your wife, all married in church, yet you speak she is very angry with you.' Her perplexity increased. 'But you are husband.' She seemed to have great difficulty in accepting Gerry's statement.

Ossie, in his second bid to gain centre stage, cleared his throat to gain her attention.

'You speak good English. Very good English. Do you speak any other languages?'

'I speak Russian. My grandfather was Russian. He was soldier in the Russo-Japanese war and he was captured. He did not go again to Russia. My grandmother was Japanese dancer then she later dance teacher. I have dancing in me. You understand?' The question was shyly directed at me.

'We say, you have dancing in your bones.'

'Ah, so.' Her eyes searched mine and there was colour in her cheeks.. 'I love very much, ballroom dancing.'

Sparky felt he was being left behind a little. 'Do you live in Yoka-ichi?'

'No, I live with my husband in Nagoya. I am here for special reason. Very special this thing. My husband he wants me to have a white baby.'

Her statement stunned all of us. Horoko looked at each of us in turn, evidently quite amused by our re-action. 'You think maybe this not proper?'

Eventually I stammered. 'Are you going to buy a white baby? Or adopt one?'

'Adopt?'

'Same as buy.'

'No, no, no. Must be proper, Bob.' She giggled, and then spoke like a schoolteacher talking to a class of infants. 'My husband will arrange a good gentleman, must be a Europe man, to come and honeymoon with me, maybe here in Yoka-ichi for some days. Maybe another place. This good gentleman must have white skin and light colour hair.' Slowly the humour left her face and she bit her lower lip nervously. 'I'm little afraid on this thing, Bob.'

The silence round our table roared in our ears. I was aware of a waiter serving a couple at a table in the window, tinkling Japanese music in the background and the low hum of traffic outside.

Two smiling waiters came with our order. The steaks were sizzling and served in thick cast iron plates set into wooden trays. A bowl of eggs was laid on the table and each of us had a separate serving of fried chips.

Horoko explained. 'In Japan, we break egg over the steak to cook. Or we make space on hot plate and egg cook there.' She looked at our faces. 'Maybe I tell waiter to bring egg all cooked?'

We beamed at her with Sparky leading the way by reaching for a fresh egg. 'This is Japan, we do it Japanese way.'

Smiling, Horoko stood up and bowed, ready to leave.

'I go now. I hope you very happy time in Japan. *Sayonara.*'

'I'll see you to your taxi.' I took her arm and led her outside to the line of waiting taxis. The early afternoon sun was warm on our faces.

'Where shall I tell the driver?'

She said softly. 'The Shimonada Hotel.'

'And if we come to the Shimonada Hotel at seven o'clock tonight, will you come dancing with us?'

Her hand moved to cover the slight blush that came to her cheeks. 'No, I can not do this thing. But please you come this beer garden tomorrow twelve o'clock time? I write it down, so.'

She fumbled in her handbag for a diary of sorts and scribbled something on it. She tore out the page and handed it to me. Then I watched the taxi disappear into the traffic.

I returned to my sizzling steak but found I had no appetite.

Next day Gerry and I found our way to the Beer Garden Horoko had written down for us. We sat under the horticultural splendour of overhanging grapevines, garlands of multicoloured flowers and graceful girls in floral kimonos gave us their full attention. Tranquillity reigned everywhere and Japanese music was being played softly.

A waitress approached and bowed. She looked at us. 'Please? You Bob-san? And you Gerry-san? Please, I am to speak you Horoko-san gone to honeymoon in Akita town this day. She is so very much sorry she speak goodbye.'

I glanced at my young friend, Gerry. A great treat had been snatched away from him, something that would have been another delight to tell his Betty. We sat for a moment in indecision.

Then I looked at the waitress and smiled sadly. 'We are sorry, too. Horoko was a good friend to us and now she has gone. You are very kind.'

'Thank you, Bob-san.'

'And what is your name?'

She blushed slightly and lowered her beautiful eyes. 'My name is Akiro-san'.

I smiled sweetly - and hopefully. 'Are you doing anything tonight, Akiro-san?'

DUGALD

The year was 1956.
I was twenty-six when I sat my Second Class B.O.T. Certificate in Glasgow. It was the final exam and I was sitting in the waiting room reading the Daily Mirror when Bob Crockett, one of my pals came in.

'When is your birthday, Bob? I'll read you your horoscope.'

I'll never forget what it said. Bob Crockett's horoscope read: 'No good can come from anything you put in writing this day.'

He didn't pass.

Anyway, I passed and became Second Engineer Officer and I remained Second Engineer Officer for twenty-six years until high-blood pressure ruled me out of deep sea shipping. Then I sailed as Chief Engineer, but only in coasters.

I just loved being Second. I loved 'fixing' things. Even as a child, I loved 'fixing' things and that is something that stays with me even though I'm now in my eighties.

Every lad I've met from the Western Isles of Scotland is a born seafarer. They have a natural affinity with the sea handed down from the generations before them. I include those in all departments, whether engine, deck or catering and from the highest rank to the lowest 'gopher'. Almost without exception, they are seafarers that rise quickly in the ranks.

Dugald was the exception. On the good ship, 'City of Swansea', he was our first trip Seventh Engineer Officer, a gangling six-footer with a great mop of hair like an Old English sheepdog and I'm sure the inhabitants of whatever Western Isle Dugald came from were glad to see him off. To hold a conversation with him was difficult, for he had to absorb what was being said, and then a few moments would be spent thinking up how to reply, by which time he'd forgotten what had just been said.

I remember at the start of that particular trip the Chief and I were having a beer before lunch when there was a knock at the cabin door.

'That'll be the new junior with the log-book,' murmured the Chief, squinting at his cabin clock. 'COME IN!'

Nothing happened and again the door was given a knock.

'COME IN!'

A moment passed and the door was knocked again.

'COME IN, damn you!'

Then there was another knock.

Before the Chief's blood pressure hit the record books, I left the comfort of my armchair and opened the door.

Dugald was standing there with a huge smile. I took the engine room logbook from him, offered it to the Chief, keeping myself solidly between them.

With a scowl, the Chief glared at Dugald. 'Waken your ideas up, junior,' he barked. Then snatching the book from my hands he carried it over to his desk and sat with his back to us.

The smiling Dugald remained in the doorway.

'Right, Dugald,' I sighed. 'What's up?'

The smile faded and his face furrowed in concentration. 'You know these two rod things at the end of the engine that do this?' Pushing his arms out sideways from the waist, he did a version of the Twist.

'The main engine fresh water cooling pump and the main engine sea water cooling pump,' I informed him, wanting to return to my beer.

He stopped moving his left arm and pointed to his right arm.

'This one.'

'That's the main engine fresh water cooling pump.'

'Well, you know the bit that the rod goes through?'

'The gland?'

His eyes lit up and he looked at me in admiration. 'That's right, that's what the Fourth Engineer called it.'

'Well, what about it, Dugald?'

'The Fourth told me to tell you that it's hot.'

I sighed again. Extracting information from Dugald required a lot of patience. 'OK. It's hot. How hot is it, Dugald? Can you touch it with your hand?'

He frowned at me and took two hurried steps back. 'Hell, no! The flames were halfway up the back of the main engine when I came up.'

This was the Chief's first introduction to Dugald, our lowest rank in engine room staff. My experience as Second Engineer taught me many things about Chief Engineers, the first being that they don't want to know about their staff. Many Chiefs insist that Head Office put them on board so they must be thoroughly interviewed and found competent. The fact that the days of the time-served apprentices with five years of evening classes behind them no longer existed, was something Head Office had difficulty accepting. Added to that was the fact that the sea now held few attractions for the modern youngster and personnel managers were gladly accepting anyone that applied.

Or the new cadet system. Like Danny, on a previous ship, eighteen years of age, who couldn't tell the time unless the clock was digital and even that was a problem. Then there was Paul, another cadet of a similar age who had never learned the alphabet. Neither had any particular wish to learn, because it was, quote, 'all too boring.' Good cadets in an engine room, God bless them, are rare, priceless and often unappreciated.

Things always went wrong when Dugald gave a hand but at least he could tell the time and he did know the alphabet. However, objects broke, bent, fell down the bilges, became lost, fell apart, were damaged, misplaced, or cracked when he was on the job. Whatever the cause, others had to be given the task of repairing anything that Dugald had been working on. One method of repair he often applied was to repeatedly strike the offending machine part with a hammer to make it work and if it broke, he'd smile quite happily, shrug his shoulders and inform me that we should have had a new one anyway.

His wave of constant destruction never seemed to bother him. There were moments when we liked his constant good humour and accepted his limitations, but those moments were rare indeed.

For instance, Big Bill Williams, Third Engineer was frantically searching in all the storeroom cupboards for a particular spare part. He dragged out boxes, emptied tins and searched in canisters at top speed. Dugald decided to give a hand. He hauled out every container he could find in that storeroom at top speed, scattered their contents on the deck, and then replaced them hurriedly.

A bewildered Big Bill turned to him. 'What are you looking for, Dugald?'

'I don't know. I'm just giving you a hand.' With that, he found another box, poured its contents on to the deck and continued to search frantically among its contents.

Or like the time Tommy Burns, the Sixth Engineer, took a boiler gauge glass tube, slid a piece of chalk inside and used it as a giant peashooter to snipe at Dugald. That piece of chalk could really sting when it hit anyone on the back of the head. However Dugald sussed it was Tommy and retaliated

He fitted a piece of chalk into a spare boiler gauge glass tube and connected it to the drainpipe of one of the main engine starting air bottles. The air pressure inside a main engine starting air bottle is 600lbs/sq. in. The pressure behind a bullet fired from a Lee-Enfield army rifle is only 88 lbs/in. When Tommy appeared round the far end of the engine room, Dugald fired his 'peashooter'. The chalk hit the oil pressure gauge on the boiler fuel pump and it smashed as if it had been struck by a hand hammer. A fine column of black boiler fuel sprayed high and wide over the engine room's clean white paintwork and cascaded on to the engine room floorplates.　　Engineers, donkeymen, greasers and wipers struggled and slithered on the slippery deck before one of them managed to shut it off.　Dugald remained the amused onlooker while this was happening.

'You great stupid clown,' I roared. 'If that chalk had hit the Sixer it could have killed him!　There's six hundred pounds per square inch air pressure in these bottles!'

Dugald nodded, quite pleased with events.

'Yes, I know,' he beamed at me. 'But it's a lot better than just blowing down the tube, isn't it?'

Tommy never used his 'peashooter' again.

On one occasion we were berthed at a jetty on the River Hoogli, somewhere below Hasting's Moorings in Calcutta.　Across the jetty from us lay a Dutch cargo ship with a complement of thirty-something stalwart officers and crew who played football.　This formidable force had gained a reputation round the Indian coast and was looking for more honours.

Three of them invited themselves on board our ship with each man carrying cans of Allsops, Heineken, and Groltz, to be met with us and an assortment of Tetley's, Tennents and Newcastle Brown Ales.

When the last beer was downed and the last Dutchman had gone we found ourselves contracted to play against them on that Saturday afternoon at three o'clock on a local football pitch.

Excitement ran high as Saturday approached, everybody was involved and even our Indian crew were coming along to cheer us to victory. Ideas and opinions, questions and answers were on everyone's lips on the subject of football and there was no shortage of enthusiasm or optimism. No one even momentarily entertained the thought that we might lose.

At two-thirty the Dutch appeared on the deck of their ship, each player immaculately turned out in a green and orange strip, with snow white shorts, orange socks and the latest in soccer footwear. Their goalkeeper was dressed entirely in orange with a black cap and white gloves.

Not one of our team had an item of football attire. Our footwear consisted of engine room shoes bound up in tape, and our shorts were certainly not our best ones. Still our hopes were high, we were full of the David and Goliath spirit, the Dunkirk spirit and a spirit made in Scotland's distilleries. We were 'The Invincibles'.

The Dutchmen pointed at us and doubled up with laughter as they trooped down their gangway and we trooped down ours. The one carrying the ball was halfway down when he contemptuously tossed it on to the jetty towards us.

Dugald let out a whoop, elbowed and pushed his way through the others and gave the ball a mighty kick that sent it heavenwards, over the end of the jetty and far out into the fast flowing River Hoogli. We watched it until it disappeared down the far reaches of the river.

Dismayed, we silently returned to our respective ships.

In the months that followed I chose Dugald's jobs and duties with great care, selecting tasks where he could do minimum damage to the engines and others.

Our five-month trip was almost over. We were having our 'smoko' in the duty mess and the ship was approaching the Clyde when the Chief came round to enquire who was coming back next trip.

He left Dugald to the last and then pointed his pencil at him.

'What, me, Chief?' Dugald beamed at all of us. 'Aye, I'll come back right enough, Chief. Och aye, I'll do it, but just to please you and Bob, but you'll have to promise me the Fourth Engineer's job first.'

Dugald was not promoted to Fourth Engineer nor was he invited to come back to the ship. He wasn't even invited to come back to the company.

I do sincerely hope that somewhere on the world's vast oceans Dugald is cheerfully spreading destruction and misfortune among the engineering officers he sails with.

I just have no wish to be one of them.

Bob Jackman

GHOSTS

We'd left Vancouver at 1900 hours on a wet and windy day and most of us had adjourned to the bar for a well-earned beer.

'Did you change the cinema box, Sparky?'

There was a worldwide system where MN ships were supplied with cinema projectors and could exchange films in various ports. The films came three in a box and one of our Radio Officer's greatest responsibilities was to ensure the films were changed at every opportunity. As a perk, he was placed in command of all things cinematographic and had the privilege of selecting the films we were to see.

'Yes! Yes! Yes! And I got the one called 'The Ghost Walks'. It's got a five star rating and I've heard about it before. There's also a cowboy with John Wayne and the other's a Norman Wisdom comedy.'

Wee Tommy Dott, our Fourth Engineer, was a film fanatic.

'Man, that's real cool! That one, 'The Ghost Walks' put the 'heebie-jeebies' up the audiences at that Cannes Film Festival thing a couple of years back. It got the kybosh from that General Release thing and can only be shown privately under special licence. It must be a real goer.'

Mad Willie, our Third Engineer, was doing a spell as bartender. The Captain leaned towards him a little. 'Mad Willie, translation, please?'

'It seems it's a very realistic horror movie about the supernatural,' whispered Mad Willie, 'banned from public viewing and apparently it meets with our Radio Officer's approval.'

'Thank you, Mad Willie.' He turned to look at the others and raised his voice a little. 'Well, gentlemen, tomorrow being Saturday, I suggest we show this ghost film tomorrow night. It's much too late to organise everything tonight. Yes, much too late. Tomorrow night, yes. Everyone agreed?'

Captain Martin being Captain Martin, no one dared disagree.

He left. Talk at the bar was quite general and four of us began a game of doubles on the dartboard.

'I really fancy seeing this ghost picture tomorrow night. It's a WOW! That's why I picked it specially.' Young Sparky looked round us for comments.

'There's no such thing as a ghost.' Jamie, our Chief Steward, spoke while waiting his turn at the dartboard. 'It's all a load of rubbish,' then hastily added, 'I admit it could be entertaining rubbish, of course.'

Andy Ryder, the Chief Electrician, said quietly; 'Maybe so, Jamie, but I remember hearing that no one has ever stayed a night in the Second Engineer's cabin on board the 'British Hussar' though dozens of fellows tried it. All the engineers have moved down a cabin and anyone who wanted the Second's cabin could have it.'

Jamie snorted. 'I'd sleep in it for a bet. No ghost would chase me out of a good cabin.'

'So,' Andy retorted. 'You admit there are such things as ghosts?'

'Or would you have sailed on the 'City of Benares?' Joe Cochran, our Chief Engineer, asked quietly as he studied the bottom of his empty beer glass.

'A City Line ship? Anytime. There was never anything wrong with John Ellerman's ships. What was wrong with her?'

Joe watched his glass being re-filled before replying. 'She was City Line's only two funnelled ship, built in Barclay Curle's Yard on the Clyde during the war. The men working on her never liked her. There were always accidents. Too many accidents, too many things going wrong for no reason and men were glad to get off her. If some men were working overtime at night they heard strange noises in places where there shouldn't have been any noises. Plumbers and joiners working in the accommodation wouldn't work past five thirty. Finally she was completed and Barclay's were glad to be rid of her. She took on a cargo at Princes Dock and joined a convoy at the Tail of the Bank. She was torpedoed two days later and sank like a brick with all hands off the coast of Ireland.' He pointed a finger at Jamie to press his point. 'City Line never built another two funnel ship.'

I paused before taking my turn at the dartboard.

'Well, I didn't believe in ghosts until I sailed as Fourth on a Nourse Line ship called the 'Megna' and had a ghost on the eight-to-twelve watch with me. I did a ten-month trip, a month's leave, then a twelve-month trip. I became quite used to this chap sometimes appearing between ten and eleven-thirty on the night watch. He always seemed to keep his distance from me, though. The Chief used to go bananas when I mentioned him.'

'Aye, but did anyone else ever see your ghost?' Jamie wanted to know. He needed confirmation.

'Quite a few. My Indian greaser on watch with me for one and, like me, he saw him regularly. So did the donkeyman on the boilers. We also had an Irish fifth engineer called John Patrick Bernard Aloysius Ignatius Quintus McMahon who saw this strange chap standing at the engine room desk one night at sea. The chap turned and walked into the storeroom. Charlie dashed after him...'

'Charlie?'

'With a name like 'John Patrick Bernard Aloysius Ignatius Quintus McMahon' we had to call him 'Charlie'. Anyway, Charlie dashed into the storeroom and it was empty. We were at sea, the storeroom was about ten-foot square *and it was empty*. Charlie described him in detail. Said he was my height, scrawny, bald on top and wearing a leather belt round the waist of his boiler suit. It was the same fellow I first kept meeting on my watch weeks later.'

The others looked at each other, uncertain how to take my story. Again it was my turn at the dartboard. I pointed my finger at Jamie for emphasis. 'The Chief went bananas when I told the others.'

'You've already said that!' Jamie was becoming irritated with the facts piling against him.

Eight bells ended Jolly Roger the Mate's 4-8 watch on the bridge. Three minutes after eight the smoke room door opened and his huge bulk waddled in with a sandwich in each hand and his mouth full.

'The Chief used to go bananas when you mentioned what, dear Bob?' He turned to the bar. 'A beer, please, Mad Willie.'

'My 8-12 engine room watch on one ship had a ghost. It was the only ghost I've ever sailed with. That has never happened in any other ship I've been on, before or since. The Chief knew something about it, probably from old log sheets or company's letters and he went off the deep end any time I mentioned it.'

'Poppycock, I say, pure poppycock! It is all imagination and auto-suggestion. People who believe in ghosts also believe in Santa Claus. Yes, Santa Claus.'

But the topic of conversation that evening remained on the subject of 'ghosts'.

Next morning Lecky was repairing a blown fuse in the galley when Jamie, the Chief Steward approached him. They confided in each other about strange experiences they'd had or heard about. It was the same with all the others. Everyone had seen or heard something uncanny, or unexplainable, at some time in their lives. Beers before dinner were accompanied with even more stories of the supernatural. They continued through dinner and went on as the projector was fitted up and the box of films brought out. Finally, the time had come and we were ready for 'The Ghost Walks'.

Our smoke room and dining saloon formed one long room. At the after end was a door to the duty mess and inboard was the door to the pantry. The screen was fitted up beside the pantry door.

Curtains were drawn over the windows and tagged down with electrical tape to stop chinks of light escaping when the ship rolled a little.

All the officers attended the first showing of the movie, with the exception of Jolly Roger, who was on bridge watch until eight o'clock and Jamie who had his catering duties to perform. Consequently, as was the custom, they would see the second showing, sitting side by side alone in the darkened saloon.

'The Ghost Walks' was an excellent adult movie. The sheer horror of the supernatural events that were portrayed made our skins crawl and covered us in goosepimples, with few exceptions.

When it was over, we, grown men, sat back and looked at each other, wide-eyed.

'That was quite a finale,' breathed Joe, his hands trembling as he picked up his beer. We were in unanimous agreement.

'That bit at the end where the girl opens the cupboard door – WOW!'

Captain Martin agreed. 'Yes, Tommy, everybody jumped at that bit! Most frightening, indeed. And a terrific build up to that climax. Right, Sparky, rewind the film and make it ready for the second showing. Jolly Roger and Chief Steward will be here in a few minutes.' His voice shook slightly.

The rest of us hurried to the bar for cold beers to revive ourselves and steady our nerves a little.

Mad Willie, my good friend and drinking partner over many long years, was up to something, but what? It was minutes later before he felt obliged to enlighten me.

'I've a big white bed sheet in a drawer in the pantry,' he whispered, 'and when it comes to that part where the girl opens the cupboard door...' He left the rest of the sentence unsaid.

It was a few minutes after eight o'clock when the Jolly Roger appeared carrying a plate of sandwiches and a beer as usual. He flopped down beside Jamie on the settee, directly in front of the screen. 'Ready when you are and make sure you keep it in focus.'

The film started.

Even though the rest of us had seen it earlier, we stayed in the background, silently supping beer and watching. As the story unfolded, the tension mounted and the only sound was the soft whirring of the projector. Eventually it came to the finale where we saw the lovely heroine make her way down the dark corridor to the library. Tension grew as she continued in breath-taking silence to the cupboard door and stopped. She threw it open as Mad Willie crashed through the pantry door covered in his white bed sheet.

Terrific shouts and yelps sounded from all of us; beer cans and glasses hit the deck and Captain Martin fell over the coffee table. Lights were switched on and not everyone was amused. There was a lot of talking, laughing and some loud cries of outraged indignation.

Jolly Roger the Mate sat in silence, unmoved. His sandwiches lay scattered on the deck, his can of beer gurgled its contents on to the settee and he was very silent. Suddenly he shuddered and moaned.

Some moments passed, he slowly rose from the settee and walked unsteadily away from the carnage, closing the smoke room door behind him.

We looked at each other, puzzled.

'It was only a joke,' murmured Mad Willie. 'Only a joke. He hasn't got a heart problem, has he? Well, it was only a joke.'

Jamie shook his head. 'Thank you, Mad Willie, but no, not a heart problem.' With shaking hands he picked up Jolly Roger's sandwiches from the floor, put them on the plate and placed them on the bar. Then he turned to face Mad Willie. 'I think you just gave him a laundry problem.'

Bob Jackman

A TALE WELL TOLD

He didn't punctuate his sentences with 'I say', 'ghastly' or 'jolly hockey sticks' but he did speak like someone with a mouthful of toffees. He looked very smart in his blazer, cravat and gold cuff links. Also, the right side of his face was a high gloss pink and slightly distorted.

'Hello, chaps, I'm the new Chief Officer, just joined, and I thought I'd come down to the bar and let your Mr Robert Pocock get on with his packing. I'm Harold Caine, call me 'Harry' and in forty-two years I've heard every joke about hurricanes.' He shook hands with a few of us. 'Now then, all this talking has made me thirsty, can I buy a round?'

I butted in before anyone could speak. 'First drink is on the house.'

There were eight of us in the bar and there were those among us who silently bought their own beer and unashamedly accepted every one offered by others. There were the others who bought a round every time they approached the bar. The rules were made by our Bar Committee but only enforced when there were 'those among us'.

Needless to say we immediately called our new addition 'Harry' to his face and 'The Hurricane' when we spoke about him to others.

It is the absolute pinnacle of bad manners to refer to a person's disfigurement or disability at any time but even more so when he's a new man in strange company.

So our Sparky said. 'How did your face get bashed in?'

Harry studied the label on his can of beer before pouring it into his glass. He wasn't the type who drank his beer from cans like the rest of us.

'It's a long story.' He took a sip of beer and nodded his approval. 'Now that's a good beer. Dutch, isn't it? Mmm, thought so. Ah, yes, the face. Banged up a bit in the war. I don't think you want to hear about it.'

'You can have another beer on the house if it's a good story,' drawled Jim Weir, the Chief Engineer.

'Well, that's an offer I can't refuse. Royal Navy, motor torpedo boats and because I had been to Oxford they made me a Squadron Commander in charge of six boats. The fact that I read archaeology and Egyptology was not a point they considered. The War Office seemed to think that I must have brains of some sort and the fact I spoke hoity-toity English rather well was qualification enough for them to make me a Squadron Commander.'

He looked at us with a puzzled expression on the left side of his face. 'I was always surprised we won the war. I had a Chief E.R.A. or Engine Room Artificer or whatever in your language, called Johnny Carmichael. He ran his own garage in a remote village in Scotland and that boy really understood engines. He was a lot more use to the navy than I was.'

He poured the last of his can into his glass, and, our Chief Engineer acting as bartender, took away the empty can and replaced it with a fresh one from the fridge.

'On the house.'

'You are most generous, most generous indeed.' Harry paused. 'Yes, Johnny Carmichael, a boy genius. He looked after all our squadron's engines. American Pratt-Whitneys, three of them in each boat, six cylinder four-strokes, turbo-blown, converted from air-cooled to water cooled, petrol start to run on paraffin and choked by manual bat.'

Chief and I looked at each other. 'Manual bat?'

Harry explained. 'The Pratt-Whitneys were a modification of a modification and the only choke you had for starting up was by holding something like a table tennis bat over the air intake of each blighter until it started. Still, mustn't complain. Spanking along at over thirty knots on a calm sea is really barreling along in any man's navy.'

'What torpedoes did you carry?' Our own Captain Stott was not a lover of engines.

'We carried two torpedoes each. Powered by Vickers Electric 1105's with 800pounder C.D.'s. CD's are contact detonators. We carried nothing else. Not even a damned catapult.'

His voice became a little quieter. We were all quiet, waiting for him to continue with his story. His eyes were focussed on the top of his beer can as if seeing things from the past.

'You remember the Tirpitz? At that time, the Tirpitz was our navy's biggest worry. She was safely tucked away in a Norwegian fjord and guarded like the crown jewels. The RAF ran a few suicide missions and got blasted out of the skies every time by anti-aircraft guns or Jerry fighters. The Tirpitz had already played merry

Hell with two Murmansk convoys and we couldn't afford losses like that.'

'That would be early 1943.' Captain Stott was putting in his bit of supporting knowledge.

'February and March, 1943. Sea temperatures were so low that men died within a couple of minutes of hitting the water when their ship went down. And they nearly all went down.'

Harry suddenly turned and looked at all of us in turn, his voice edged with excitement. 'Suddenly we heard that the Tirpitz was out of fuel and a tanker was on its way to fill her up again. Stop that tanker and you'd stopped the Tirpitz we were told. Tally-ho and yoicks and all that sort of stuff. We were in Montrose in Scotland and could be off in minutes, all six boats raring to go. News came up that we might just intercept the tanker at such and such a point if we could maintain thirty knots. There was a light haze on the water when we left but it was thickening all the time until it looked as if we were pushing our way through cotton wool. I could hear the others close behind me but we couldn't even see each other. I had the horrible thought of what would happen if we all ran slap-bang into the side of a damned ship.'

He took out his handkerchief and wiped his face.

'Sorry, chaps, I tend to get a bit shook up when it all comes back to me.'

We sat quietly and some of us had another beer to give him time to recover.

'How long did it take you to reach the meeting point?' Sparky asked, interrupting Harry's silence.

'Approximately three hours, if I remember correctly. It was the most amazing thing you ever saw in your life. We came out of the fog into a circle of bright sunlight and the tanker we had little hope of finding was right in front of us. About two miles away and right in front of us! It was nonchalantly steaming along in brilliant sunlight with the Norwegian coast in the background.'

Harry's hand shook and he pointed to spirits on display. 'A Scotch if you would be so kind, Chief. Make it a large one.'

The Chief poured him a double Scotch.

'Water?'

Harry shook his head.

'We headed for the tanker in brilliant sunlight and were still a mile from it when a German destroyer came out of the fog. It was all over in minutes. We fired our torpedoes in the general direction of the tanker and scampered for our lives but we were caught like rats in a barrel. The destroyer picked us off one at a time, with ease. Our boat just made it into the fog again when she was hit. She was the last one to be hit.' He touched the side of his face. 'That's when I received this. The amazing thing is that a piece of wreckage snagged on one of our mooring ropes and hung behind the ship like a sea anchor or drogue and kept the boat on a straight course. The Pratt-Whitney's kept running. Evidently she ran straight up on to the beach somewhere on the East Coast of Scotland. I knew nothing about all this. I was unconscious from the time we were hit until I woke up in Raigmore Hospital in Inverness with the side of my head somewhat caved in. These poor medical chaps, surgeons, doctors, specialists and bone experts spent weeks taking the dents out and gave me this face. I may not be the handsomest man around but I'm handsome enough. I was the only one that survived that raid. I lost twenty-three good mates in that one night. Twenty-three died in a matter of minutes. Later, I heard later that one torpedo blew off the tanker's rudder, she couldn't move and the RAF finished her off. Well, that's the whole darned story.'

I put a hand on his shoulder. 'Have a Scotch with me, Harry. It's nice to have you on board.'

Sparky looked puzzled at him, puzzled.

'Harry?'

'Yes, Sparky?'

'They've called you 'Hurricane' for forty-two years?

'Yes, Sparky.'

'You are forty-two years old?'

'Yes, Sparky.'

'Harry, this is 1976. You were born in 1934?'

'Yes, Sparky.'

'So in 1944, when the torpedo boats went after the tanker and the Tirpitz was holed up in Norway, you must have been just ten years old?'

'Well, nine, actually.'

Bob Jackman

A DUTCH AND SCOTTISH MIXTURE

I remember the old 'Cape Howe' with a lot of affection. Every shipping company should have a 'Cape Howe', an old ship that responded to a little bit of care and attention and never let her engineers down.

However, it seems the 'Howe' didn't like some of the office staff.

When I joined her in Terminus Quay in Glasgow, the staff from Head Office in Buchanan Street had invaded the smokeroom and the ship's officers were not invited to their party. Seafaring staff were of little consequence in their eyes.

The 'Howe' had returned from the hard, frozen wastes of Murmansk in Northern Russia. Her emergency generator in the steering flat had succumbed to the intense cold and her cylinder block had a beautiful crack right down the middle.

Our head marine superintendent, well under the influence of alcohol was giving a guided tour to some of the higher echelons of the office party and explaining in great detail how such a fault might have been avoided.

I kept in the background, no one knew who I was, having only joined an hour earlier.

'There was no treatment – hic - supplied by the makers to check the strength of the machine's anti-freeze.' He stepped back a little for effect, and then repeated his words. 'There was no chemical supplied to check – hic - the strength of the anti-freeze.'

There are times in one's life when it is a good idea to keep one's mouth shut. This, most certainly, was one of them.

I coughed and the heads turned.

'I think, personally, being an Engineer, I would have taken an empty beer can, filled it with a sample of the generator's cooling water, and put it in the ship's freezer flat to see if it froze.'

I thought he was going to hit me. The others thought it was funny but he didn't. He never liked me after my statement. But then, thinking back, he never liked me before it either.

Some months later the Cape Howe was in Holland and the local authorities were holding a celebration, a celebration that snowballed quite a bit. Evidently it was Scottish troops who liberated this particular Dutch port after the Normandy landings and the Ambassador and many of the Dutch hierarchy decided to hold an anniversary party to mark the occasion. The senior officers from all British ships in port on that day were invited to attend and, of course, our senior pen pushers from head office back in the UK invited themselves.

Office staff can make or break shipping companies. Some members in our office staff were the breaking variety and there were others who were gentlemen who knew their jobs.

The Head Marine Superintendent wore a constant sneer. He cornered the Mate and his wife, the Second Mate, Sparks, the Chief Steward and myself in the ship's smokeroom and informed us on how he wanted us to behave.

'There's all kinds of toffs will be at this 'do', tonight, so you lot better behave yourselves: You in particular, Jackman.'

'It's *Mister* Jackman.'

We'd 'had words' earlier that morning and it still rankled him. But it annoyed me too. He was a five-star bully that maintained his position by being in a constant temper and soon sacked those who didn't dance to his tune. Highly competent ship's officers left to find employment elsewhere and those that had the temerity to leave could not expect good references.

I couldn't leave; I had sailed 'foreign flag' and now had to sail with any company that needed a qualified engineer. Such was the state of Merchant Navy Mismanagement in those far off days with constant battles between Unions and Companies. I still bless the Unions.

So the great shoreside event came and I think our group, office staff and ship's officers alike, was a little in awe of what we saw. Huge luxury limousines came to collect us from the ship and take us to the city hall. The police were out in force, directing traffic and people lined the streets, waving flags. Doormen in livery ushered us into the town hall, a hall so large that voices echoed as in a great cathedral. Somewhere in the background we could hear the soft skirl of bagpipes.

There were lots of ladies in evening dress, men in uniform or dinner jackets and bow ties, some with great silk sashes across their bodies and waiters weaved among them carrying trays of drinks.

An hour went by. Our super office staff was still wedged in the same tight little group, nervously in awe of the majestic splendour surrounding them. Our ship's officers were huddled in another little tight group, talking in whispers and with my hearing not what it should be due to my long years in engine rooms, I was missing quite a lot of their hushed conversation.

I grew slightly bored with their furtive whisperings and wandered off to listen to the pipers. All four stood on an outside lawn, shut off by the French windows. As they finished playing a march I moved outside to join them.

'Any o' youse yins frae Glesca?' I enquired in my broadest Glasgow accent and we were pals immediately. After a few minutes of conversation I found that they had being playing for over an hour and had no refreshment of any kind.

I sympathised. 'I'll have a wee word with someone. You might be lucky.'

I made my way to the buffet where a large area was set out for wines, beers and spirits. There were four stewards at work in the drinks section and I chose the one who was obviously in charge.

A pained expression. 'Yes, sir?'

'The bagpipe music is becoming squeaky. In fact, it's almost screechy.'

'Sir?' The eyebrows rose a few millimetres.

'You see, when the pipers' throats become dry with blowing into the bagpipes, the music goes dry as well. That's why it becomes squeaky.'

His eyes smiled. 'Ah! Would some whisky assist them, sir?'

'Every half hour?'

'Most certainly, sir: Every half hour as you suggest, sir.' This time the smile almost reached the corners of his mouth. I watched him pour four large Scotches and set off in the direction of the French windows. On his return, he looked at me, his left eye flickered slightly and he smiled.

I was beginning to enjoy myself. From past experience I knew the Dutch to be a warm friendly people but tend to hesitate in making the first move towards strangers.

The superintendents and my fellow officers were still two separate groups that spoke in whispers and then only to each other. They made no effort to socialise with their Dutch hosts though they did partake of their host's refreshments quite freely.

The evening was moving on when I saw a little old lady standing alone as if ready to leave. She had a red silk stole over a gold evening dress and a sequin studded evening bag in her left hand. Probably well into her eighties, I thought, but she must have been a beautiful lady in her day. She had all the charm and poise of the aristocracy.

'Excuse me, madam, but it isn't safe for a beautiful lady to be alone in a place like this when there are so many sailors about.'

Her eyes widened and she giggled. 'Oh dear, will you protect me?'

'You're Scots!' I exclaimed.

'Yes, I'm Scots. From Aberdeen.'

So I introduced myself. We talked and she told me her son had brought her here as a treat but she felt it was time to go home. It had been a long evening for her and she was a little tired.

'Ah, here he is, at last.'

A tall fair-haired gentleman approached us, resplendent in an orange sash, evening jacket and medals on his left shoulder.

'Jacob, this is Bob. Bob so gallantly protected me from all the wandering sailors lurking about when you went off and deserted me. Bob, this is my son, Jacob.'

I soon found Jacob to be extremely courteous but he lacked his mother's ready wit and sense of humour.

We talked, then after a few minutes he said, 'It was good meeting you, Bob, but we must go. My Mother is tired.'

She leaned towards me, gave my arm a squeeze and kissed me on the cheek.

'You are my knight in shining armour,' she smiled, wrinkling her nose at me.

Suddenly Jacob's face lit up. 'Mother, give me a moment to introduce Bob to General MacKenzie.' He turned to me. 'Alisdair is Scottish, too, I think you should meet him.'

So I was introduced to General Alisdair MacKenzie, then Jacob and his mother left. At the door, she turned and waved to me.

The general pulled on the points of his moustache and drew himself up to his full height as we watched them go.

'She's Scots, from Aberdeenshire, and a very fine lady.'

'A very fine lady indeed. You're Scots, too, General?'

'Aye, born near Inverary.'

So our conversation went on with him talking about his life in the army and me elaborating on the highlights and stresses of a life in the Merchant Navy.

I noticed our company's marine superintendents were not oblivious to my companion and, conceited ass that I am, I gloried in it.

General MacKenzie suddenly switched topics. 'I wanted the Ambassador to see a bit of Scotland so last August we went to Scourie in Sutherlandshire and fished the best lochs there. Never even saw a damned trout. The annoying part is that I had been bragging about how the lochs are packed full of the damned things.' He shook his head in mock despair. 'And we never even *saw* one! Dammit, Bob, he laughed at it but it made me look a proper idiot.'

'What made you look a proper idiot, Alisdair?'

I found we were now joined by the Dutch Ambassador himself and I was being introduced. All the guests there had their eyes focussed on our little group in the centre of the great hall.

Alisdair went on. 'I was telling Bob about our fishing holiday in Scotland, when you and I caught exactly nothing. We never even touched a fish.'

Our host smiled. 'Well, let's try again this year, Alisdair.'

I took a deep breath. 'Might I make a suggestion, gentlemen?'

'Of course, please do, Bob.'

' If you are going to fish in the Scourie, Kinlochbervie or the Riconich area of Sutherlandshire in August, I recommend you use a normal cast of three flies, number eights or even bigger, with the tail fly weighted. Use a sinking line and fish deep, right to the bottom. Trout lie in the deepest water in hot, sunny weather and the lochs are as deep as the mountains are high.'

The Ambassador and the General looked at each other then looked at me.

I explained, smiling. 'My sister's husband is a MacKay of Sutherland.'

From then, the conversation was on trout fishing and every angler knows a dozen good stories on that subject. We laughed our way through all of them.

Eventually the celebrations drew to a close. Final speeches were made, the Ambassador had something to say, it was all over and the guests politely applauded.

General Alisdair MacKenzie and I warmly shook hands, and then I made my way to join my own group of ship's officers.

'Jackman!'

It seemed our head marine superintendent wanted a word.

So I turned and walked back to him and his disciples. He was fuming and his face was a violent red.

'You were talking and laughing with the Ambassador. You were talking to the Ambassador and that army general fellow.'

I looked at all their faces before my eyes returned to our head marine superintendent.

'The Ambassador and Alisdair were talking to me.'

His nose came to within twelve inches of mine and I smiled pleasantly. 'And just what could you find to talk about with a Dutch Ambassador and a Dutch army general, Jackman?'

'Oh, nothing much. They were hoping I'd go with them on a fishing holiday, up in the North of Scotland, for a week or two: The three of us together sometime in early August. But I don't think I'll bother, really. You never know what things like that can lead to.'

I smiled at each of them in turn and nonchalantly returned to the others.

THE THIRD'S WIFE

I loved being Second Engineer. When I was very young and one of my playmates broke a toy they always brought it to me to fix. I grew up fixing things. During my five-year apprenticeship on the Clyde I made time to make model steam engines, cigarette lighters and designed special tools for special jobs. In my final year in the Engine Works I worked overtime and weekends at every opportunity and completed five years at evening classes. Consequently, when I went to sea I rose to the rank of Second Engineer rather rapidly.

I had, however, some difficulty in accepting that there were thousands that didn't share my enthusiasm for using tools or fixing things. Furthermore, I never had the wish to sail as Chief Engineer doing the paperwork involved in running a ship or wondering how to spend the rest of the day without getting in the way of the Second Engineer.

I loved tools and sweaty boiler suits but I also loved the beer and darts and being in a smart uniform on off-duty periods in the Officers Smokeroom. Where once I had sailed as a young Certificated Second Engineer Officer in the Merchant Navy I was rapidly becoming one of the oldest.

There came a day when the Chief's head popped round my cabin door. 'New Third Engineer coming in Gibraltar, Bob, a chap called Darel. I knew a Donny

Darel. A big hyper-active gorilla. Good worker. Evil temper. Quick with his fists.'

'Dammit! I'll be sorry to lose Big Bill Williams.'

'Bringing his wife. Newly weds. A girl, straight from a convent. So the beers are on Big Bill in Gibraltar.'

A.C. Downie was a good Chief and easy to get on with. He always spoke as if dictating telegrams. A six-foot thinking man who never flapped about anything but could eat Superintendents, Captains and Lloyd's Surveyors raw if the situation required it.

We arrived in Gibraltar, Big Bill Williams departed, Mr and Mrs Darel joined and we sailed for Port Said.

This hyperactive gorilla lived up to his description. He was down the engine room in a boiler suit within ten minutes of coming on board, saw everything, grunted his disapproval and spoke to no one. All his movements were jerky and seemingly uncontrolled. He waddled from side to side when he moved.

His wife was young and very beautiful. She had the kind of beauty that would make a priest want to kick holes in the confessional door.

At 'Full Away', I came up out of the engine room and she was standing in the middle of the Third Engineer's cabin, tentatively unpacking two suitcases. She had all the serenity and tranquillity of a Mother Superior and the beauty of a Hollywood starlet.

'Hello, Mrs Darel, welcome on board. I'm Bob, Second Engineer.'

We shook hands and she seemed to hold on to my hand a little longer than people normally do in those occasions.

'Oh, please, I am Maria.' Lovely eyes, big dark eyes like a baby deer and her voice did strange things to my knees when she spoke.

I smiled. 'Your husband won't be much longer, Maria. He has a few things to see to.'

I left her, moved into my own cabin next door and thought 'WOW!!'

The cabin wall separating the bunks in our two bedrooms was made of one-inch thick wooden blockboard. When Big Bill, the previous Third Engineer, slept next door I could hear every sound he made when he was in his bunk. If he was reading a book in bed I could even hear him turning the pages.

And they were newly-weds! I changed my sleeping arrangements from the bunk in my bedroom to the settee in my dayroom and kept the door closed between them.

As always in those far-off days, the Third Engineer and the Sixer did the 12 to 4 watch and my Junior and I took over from them at 4.00 o'clock to do the 4 to 8 watch. At no time was I aware of any humphing, bumping or ecstatic squeals coming through my bedroom bulkhead so by the end of the week I returned to sleeping in my bunk again.

Then, a week later, about two o'clock in the morning there was some humphing and bumping, grunting and squealing, coming through that one inch thick blockboard wall into my cabin, loud enough to waken me. Was our Third Engineer Officer enjoying his marital rights with his dear lady wife when he should have been down below, on watch in the engine room?

Bob Jackman

I picked up the telephone beside my bed and dialled 'engine room'.

'Hello, Third speaking.'

It was certainly Donny's voice.

I whispered. 'Hello, Donny, what's the time on the engine room clock? My clock's stopped.'

'Eight minutes past two.'

'Okay.' I hung up.

So the Third's wife had a mysterious lover? Well, good luck to the blighter, whoever he is, but that blighter was sailing in very dangerous waters.

The noises continued for some minutes longer and I returned to the settee in my dayroom with my head under a pillow.

There's an unwritten law at sea; leave the married ones alone. Strange things have happened to lovers who were caught with their trousers down and the husbands are never judged to be guilty of any action they take.

Darts are the main pastime on board. When I join a ship for the first time I buy three or four sets of darts to take with me because there's always a dartboard in the smokeroom but seldom any darts. New darts whip up interest among players and watchers. It always reaches a pitch where someone suggests we start playing for cigarettes and then my long years of experience in throwing darts at a dartboard on a moving ship stand by me well.

I enjoyed taking cigarettes off the others. The more I took off Captains, Chief Stewards and fellow officers in the Deck Department, the better I played. At the end of the night I would share my winnings with the Juniors and cadets.

Things came to pass when it was decided that we should play doubles. All the persistent losers were quickly in favour and Captain Stott's bad temper made it law. Partners were soon chosen and I was left with Donny Darel, the aggressive gorilla, as my partner.

He growled at all of us when he heard the news. 'What! Bugger off! I don't play darts. Find somebody else. I'm not playing darts. I don't get paid for playing stupid games.' Then he stormed out of the smokeroom in another of his sudden rages.

Everything went quiet. I was without a partner and there were those among us who wanted to recoup their losses from previous evenings.

She was sitting on one of the smokeroom settees, a vision of angelic chastity with her ankles crossed and her hands neatly folded on her lap.

'Maria? Will you be my partner?'

Her eyes went wide and she looked round all of us. 'But I have never played darts before. I wouldn't know what to do!' Her helpless beauty touched all our hearts and smiles of smug satisfaction passed between my fellow officers.

Walking over to where she was standing, I whispered. 'Don't worry. I'll tell you what to do. It's just a spot of fun.'

She had never thrown a dart in her life before but she could soon put a dart into, or close to, any single, double or treble I pointed to. She was a star! Do they have dartboards in convents? Was the Good Lord giving her a hand? When we won almost every game hands down she jumped up and down with childish excitement.

Our winnings amounted to nearly forty packets of cigarettes, neatly stacked on one of the smokeroom's coffee tables. That was 'big winnings' for one evening's play.

'That's twenty packets each,' I laughed, stuffing the packets into empty carton boxes. 'It's been quite a night.'

'Oh, no, Bob, please. I don't smoke, and neither does my Donny. But I'd like one packet. A souvenir of a wonderful evening.' Her voice dropped to a whisper, 'with you.'

Clutching her one packet of cigarettes she went to the smokeroom door and turned. 'Goodnight, everybody, goodnight. And thank you all for a really wonderful evening. Oh! You made me so happy. Especially you, Bob.'

Why me? I was now in my fifties, old enough to be her father and twenty years older than most of the others.

She closed the door behind her.

The cries went up from the others – 'Oh! Especially you, Bob,' 'She will be calling you 'Bob, darling' next', 'Ho! Ho! Better not let her dear husband find out, Bob.'

She was most probably just being kind to me, an old man in comparison with the others. Was it because I treated her like a lady? Also, was I not the one who introduced her to the game – and won?

It was all meant to be harmless banter but it could be a spark into a powder keg, particularly from those who were poor losers.

So I had another beer at the bar and the evening fizzled out. Those of us left locked up, put out the lights and made our separate ways to our cabins. It was then about 11.00 o'clock.

At 04.00 hours I took over the watch from the Third. The Seventh Engineer, a boy of twenty-one tender years, an innocent who had never had dirt on his hands until he joined the Merchant Navy, was my assistant on the 4 to 8 watch.

He was forcing his eyes to stay open but I could see he was having a hard struggle.

'Have you checked the bilges?'

'Mm?'

'Have you checked the engine room bilges?'

'Er, yes. All okay.'

'The tunnel well? The shaft bearings?'

He shook his head. 'Er, no, not yet.'

I paused. 'What time did you go to bed last night? And how much had you been drinking?'

Suddenly he was close to tears. I felt like a headmaster quizzing a six-foot schoolboy. God help our Merchant Navy.

'Didn't get to bed last night.'

My voice rose. 'You didn't go to bed last night! What in the hell were you up to?'

'I was in the deck cadets' cabin.' Then the words came out with a rush. 'Last night there was the Sixer and the two deck cadets and me and we were all in the deck cadets' shower room with the Third's wife, Maria, after he went on watch, all in the shower together with no clothes on and all of us doing – 'it'– with her and her loving it and wanting more and doing it in their bathroom because nobody can hear us outside their bathroom and she wanted you there as well, Second, because she likes you...'

I turned away and ran my eyes over all the gauges on the main engine control panels without really seeing them. The picture of four lusty young men and a very co-operative Maria fornicating most of the night naked in a shower room was imprinted on my brain: The Maria who was so childishly excited at winning at darts: Doing 'it' with the four youngsters.

'She likes you, Second...'

He was standing fidgeting beside the engine room desk, frightened of what I might say or do.

I sighed. 'Go up top, soak your head and face under a cold water tap, don't dry yourself and come back on watch. That'll keep you wakened. And as for that business with the Third's wife, keep your mouth shut and pray to God none of you get caught.' I spoke slowly to emphasise my next words. 'If that big brute of a Third finds out, he will kill you.' I paused for emphasis. 'I mean, he will *kill* you.'

So, my Junior, the Seventh Engineer Officer, staggered round most of our 4 to 8 watch with a trembling lower lip, scared out of his mind and eager to please.

Finally, at 8.00 o'clock, the engine room watch was over and my Junior went straight to his bed. I showered, dressed and went for a breakfast of fried eggs, bacon, toast and coffee in the dining saloon though I wasn't really hungry.

Just as the steward was serving me, Mr Donny Darel stormed in and looked most annoyed with me. The saloon was quite deserted. He sat next to me, the Third Engineer's usual seat at mealtimes.

He cleared his throat and it sounded ominous.

'My wife...'

I thought, 'Here we go. Big trouble.'

'Aye, Donny?'

'Last night...'

My hand shook slightly as I poured myself a coffee. 'What about last night?'

He repeated. 'Last night you were with her.'

'Yes. My partner at darts. We won forty packets of cigarettes.'

'I mean after that!' His voice gritted, pushing his face close to mine.

The bacon in my mouth became a bit chewy and my coffee was still too hot to drink and my cup rattled in its saucer. 'After what, Donny?'

'She told me all about it. Everything!'

I put my knife and fork down on my plate, taking care not to drop them and looked him straight in the eye. Our noses were inches apart. 'Donny, tell me. What do you mean by 'everything'?'

His scowl deepened. 'She helped you win forty packets of cigarettes at the darts and you only gave her one packet for herself! One packet! You took advantage of my innocent young wife!'

I said nothing but my whole body went so limp with relief I nearly slid off the chair and under the table. Instead, I returned to trying to swallow my bacon and eggs.

'Donny, I got news for you. Oh, boy! Oh boy! Oh boy! Have I got news for you?'

Bob Jackman

But I have kept it a secret. Well, up to now, that is.

HAGGIS POWER

We arrived in Murmansk and liked it. Weather conditions were appalling even by Russian standards, but a bus was supplied by the shipping agents to take us to and from the Seamen's Club. There were many young hosts and hostesses, eager to talk of their world and ask about ours. All the girls were beautiful with clear, clean skins and eyes that smiled so readily. The Club also boasted a well-stocked bar and a shop that sold useful items for seafarers.

Our cargo of coal lying on the dockside had been soaked with a fall of snow a few days earlier and the sudden drop in temperature had caused the mounds of wet coal to freeze into rows of solid black pyramids. It seemed our two-day stay might take longer than we thought.

The days passed slowly. Danny Dyce, our Chief Steward Extra-ordinaire, became one of the club's most regular visitors and, like all good Chief Stewards, he could achieve anything. A Chief Steward armed with a bottle of Scotch in a plain wrapper in a Seamen's Club was often better informed than the Captain with a stuffed briefcase at the shipping office.

'We're sailing on Saturday morning,' a snow covered Danny informed us as he swept into the smoke room. 'And furthermore,' he continued, taking a deep breath,

'I've arranged for the Seamen's Club staff to come on board on Friday afternoon.'

'Friday? That's tomorrow!' Val, Fourth Engineer quickly informed us.

Hughie, Third Engineer, yelled. 'Right first time! See that? He's clever, our Val!'

We had a complement of fourteen officers, most of them engineers in their twenties and most of Friday morning was spent preparing for the arrival of our guests, with Danny in charge.

The conditions laid down were as follows; the ladies were to stay in the smoke room and not allowed any 'guided tours' with ship's officers. The cadets' accommodation, washroom and toilet were for the use and convenience of the ladies only. If any of the club staff were found taking alcohol the entire group would be returned to the Seamen's Club and all would be reprimanded. The escort would be obeyed at all times.

Escort? What kind of 'escort'? Even the enterprising Danny was unsure.

'Probably some old woman that enjoys her vodka,' Hughie said. 'I don't think she'll be anything to worry about.'

They arrived. Eight excited girls, three young men and one fat slob in his mid-forties. Being heavily clad against the fierce weather outside, it was a few minutes before hats, coats, mittens and snow boots were dispensed with and they settled down to look at everything and everybody. The slob was dressed in a fur collared military-style greatcoat, a fur hat, quilted jodhpurs of sorts, jackboots and an army blouse. Everything he wore had a red star emblazoned on it.

Danny produced an array of soft drinks and the fat slob reached out and snatched one out of Danny's hand to read the label.

'No vodka?'

Danny smiled sweetly. 'No, nothing alcoholic. That is one of the conditions we have to abide by and we have agreed to it.'

'Huh!'

He flopped down to sit beside me, surveyed everyone and everything in the smoke room then pushed his face close to mine.

'You Second Engineer Officer?' He sprayed and slobbered a bit when he spoke.

'Yes.'

I leaned away, but I was wedged against the smoke room bookcase. He leaned even closer and tapped his chest.

'See me? Me Second Engineer Officer.'

'That's nice.' I forcefully pushed against him so that I could sit upright again. It didn't enter this slob's head that I would have appreciated some space between us; anything over twenty-five yards would have been ideal. There were sympathetic looks on the faces of the others but short of standing up and giving him a push, I couldn't think of anything. Siberian prison camps were a lot nearer than our House of Commons and the inmates are not much nicer.

Danny meantime produced two large plastic jars of 'Quality Street' chocolates and offered them round the group. There were looks of complete rapture on their faces as each guest took a chocolate and put it in their

---

mouth. Eyes closed, they savoured the moment and hands shyly returned to the jar for another.

The fat slob had picked up one of the jars and held it wedged between his knees, thereby claiming it as his own. He was slobbering with about four chocolates in his mouth and unwrapping a fifth when he turned to me again.

'What engine you have? Eh?'

'Diesel'

'Diesel?'

His spray was now chocolate flavoured when he spoke. I was glad I wasn't a triple expansion superheated steam job with Foster-Wheeler boilers. I was angrily levering him upright again when Hughie came to my rescue.

'You're a Second Engineer Officer? How would you like to see what a good engine room looks like?' He asked the slob. 'It's very modern, full of new ideas.'

The jaws stopped moving with the mouth remaining in the open position. He looked from Hughie to me, then back to Hughie.

'British top secret ideas,' Hughie whispered.

The jar of 'Quality Street' was laid at his feet and Hughie left the smoke room with the Slob waddling after him. When the door closed behind them, some of the girls immediately jumped to their feet and slipped over to me. There were whispers of; 'so sorry – he is always so terrible – none of us like him'.

A hand bearing a tranquillising double Scotch wriggled through between the girls and I made its contents disappear in three gulps.

'Thanks, Val.' I didn't need to see the face to know who slipped me the whisky.

Some of them changed places and this time I found myself with a sympathetic young lady by my side. We were becoming friendlier by the minute when Hughie and the slob returned.

He yanked the sweet young thing out of her seat and again returned to his former position of leaning against me.

'You engine no good engine. Russia engine good engine. You engine ver' no good engine.'

I could see Hughie's face pleading with me to stay calm, pleading with me not to punch the slob's nose. I smiled back at him pleasantly and turned my attention to the idiot child.

'In Russia engine you use fuel oil?'

'Da. Fuel oil.'

'Maybe coal?'

'Coal in steam engine ship,' he nodded, sure of his facts.

'But not haggis?' His face moved back three inches to study me more closely.

'Haggis? What this haggis?'

At various times in our sea careers, Hughie and I have been quite telepathic with each other. This was one of those times. He pointed an accusing finger at me and scowled. 'That is top secret information, Second Engineer Officer Jackman. It's only for Britain and America!' The words were ground out between his clenched teeth.

'I thought...'

Hughie raised his voice a little but his accusing finger remained pointing at me.

'Top secret!'

The fat slob's jaws stopped munching his 'Quality Street' and the silence was deafening. He couldn't make up his mind whether to look at Hughie or me. Finally, he looked at me.

'Haggis?'

Val could never leave well alone. 'The Chinese got permission from Billy Connelly...'

'Billy Connelly...?'

'Yes, Billy Connelly, British Ambassador for Partick and other Allied Forces in Europe. Haggis for all, he used to say. If every ship had a haggis we would never need fuel oil again.'

'They lit all the street lights in Glasgow for a whole year with one haggis and now they've shut down the atomic power station in the Locarno Ball Room,' Hughie whispered to the fat slob.

He believed every word we said. His Quality Street had spilled on to the deck as his trembling fingers wrote something feverishly in a leather bound notebook. Suddenly he was up and moving to the far corner of the smoke room to continue to write.

After a few minutes he came over to me and squashed down beside me again.

'This haggis? How big this haggis thing?'

I didn't speak but I moved my hands as if I was clutching a coconut. All other questions met with a shake of my head and Hughie kept Val quiet.

Suddenly the slob jumped to his feet, snapped his notebook shut and clapped his hands.

'We go back to Seamen Club now. I have business.' He had a smug look on his face as if he'd outwitted us in some way.

Our visitors took their time putting on their heavy weather clothes and he didn't like the delay.

Then Danny, our Chief Steward Extra-Ordinaire appeared with a large box neatly wrapped in coloured paper and tied with a huge bow.

'Thank you! Thank you! Thank you, for coming to our ship and bringing so much happiness with you. We are sorry we must leave you tomorrow morning but we give you something to remember us by. Tomorrow night is 'Kiltie Night', a special celebration to commemorate when 'The Cheeky Forty' won a decisive battle against 'The San Toy' at Glasgow Cross so many years ago. There is a present for each of you in this box, but...' he paused for emphasis, 'we ask you to keep with our traditions. The box must only be opened on a Saturday evening when the first stars appear in the sky and only opened by an important committee of Russian Naval Personnel and important persons connected with power stations. All government officials. OK?'

'Oh, yes! Yes,' the Fat Slob cried. 'I am important, I can arrange it all. I shall bring the heads of all departments! I shall take the box! I shall open it for them to see.'

Danny handed the box to him. 'I place this box in your keeping, my friend. Your name will be long remembered.'

We waved them off. We stood out on deck in the sub-zero temperatures until the bus turned the corner at the end of the sheds then dashed inside for double tots of black rum to thaw out.

Finally, when my blood began to defrost, I turned to Danny.

'That was a very clever little speech you made. Remembering the 'The Cheeky Forty' and 'The San Toy' and making up a 'Kiltie Night' business.'

Hughie butted in. 'And the box is not to be opened until the stars come out this Saturday?'

'Yes, 'Kiltie Night'. I just made that up, actually.'

'And it is only to be opened by an important person? Why?' Val wanted to know.

Danny watched his rum swirl around in his glass.

'That bad animal couldn't wait to get ashore with this great secret about haggis being a new revolutionary fuel for ships and he'd tell every important person he met. We sail in the morning. By the time the first stars come out he'll have some VIPs lined up to open the box and hand out the twelve presents. The youngsters that came to our party would each receive their present.'

He finished his rum and laid down his glass for refilling.

'A very kind thought, Danny,' I smiled and everybody nodded in agreement. 'What did you give them?'

'I presented each of them with a tin of haggis. Each tin has a picture of a haggis, steaming gently on a dinner plate and a label with the necessary instructions how to cook it.'

Our cheer could have easily been heard three ship lengths away

I placed one hand solemnly on our noble Chief Steward's shoulder and we all raised our glasses to him.

'Danny Dyce, we salute you.'

SATAN

After dinner each day, the Captain, the Second Mate, Sparks and I played doubles at darts until eight o'clock. This was a set routine that had developed over our months of sailing together.

Then came a day when two new officers joined and two officers left, having completed their term of duty. Those that joined were a first trip engine room cadet called Stetten and an old pal of mine, a Third Engineer Officer called Hughie McPhail.

'That cadet is trouble, Bob. I met up with him at Heathrow thinking we would travel out together. On board the plane he got stroppy with one of the air hostesses. Well, I warned him, then the plane's Chief Steward had to come and warn him about his conduct and keeping his voice down. In the end I left him and moved to another seat. That boy is trouble and he's only a kid.'

Hughie was a gentleman in any man's language but if the Pope himself condemns any one of my staff, I still check him out for myself.

It didn't take long.

We sailed from Capetown on the following afternoon and after dinner that evening, we, the Darts Team, were back to playing our matches as per usual when Stetten walked into the smokeroom.

By the bar was a cassette player with dozens of tapes of pop music. He switched on to pop music at full volume, while snapping his fingers and rocking his head.

I walked over and turned the volume down a bit. 'We don't like it that loud, sonny.'

He pushed my hand away. 'That's what it's here for, isn't it?' he growled.

I moved to take my turn at the board and he immediately turned the cassette player up to full volume again.

This time the Captain walked over and switched the machine off. 'You will leave it OFF,' he thundered.

But within five minutes it was back on again, and, in the end, I'm ashamed to say, we gave up playing darts and he continued playing the cassette recorder at full volume.

Consequently the other officers would have nothing to do with him and he looked at them with contempt and derision. Things had to come to a head.

The Chief Engineer was a long served 'Company's man' that, when informed of any situation, 'didn't want to get involved'. Or if anyone mentioned the 'engines' he would fly into a tantrum. He was the kind who was a pathetic failure as Second Engineer, wouldn't go back to Third, couldn't quit, so desperately memorised the textbooks until he became Chief.

However, the day arrived when most of us had had enough of Satan as Stettin was now called, and I was ordered to bring him up to the Captain's office where the Chief Engineer and the Captain intended to have strong words with him.

When Satan and I arrived, the atmosphere in the Captain's office seemed to crackle and I could feel dark thunderclouds hanging in the air.

'Right, Mr Stetten.' The Captain spoke through gritted teeth. 'Since joining this vessel...'

But Satan was paying no attention to the Captain. He saw a 'girlie' magazine on top of a bookcase, walked passed the Captain and picked it up, then spread himself out on the settee and started flicking through the pages.

The Captain's face turned purple and he raised his clenched fists.

'YOU...!'

With seeing Satan every working day I had anticipated something like this could happen and rapidly stepped in between them.

'Calm yourself, Captain. Just calm yourself. Softly, now, calm yourself.'

He was quivering with rage but had he, the Captain of a British ship, struck a young cadet in the presence of two senior officers, all three of us would be dragged through every court in the United Kingdom and found guilty in each one.

Meanwhile our intrepid Chief Engineer stood with his mouth open, looking blankly at each of us in turn, silently struggling to absorb the scene before him.

The Captain stretched his arm beyond me, shaking a finger pointed at Satan.

'GET HIM OUT OF HERE!'

I took Satan by the collar with one hand, held the Captain off with the other and retreated backwards out of the Captain's office. At the door, Satan shrugged off my grip on his collar, swore at me in the foulest language and sauntered off, still clutching the Captain's girlie magazine.

Radio messages flew between Captain and Head Office over the next few days with Head Office making volumes of empty promises that they had no intention of keeping.

It was just about midnight thirty-six hours later when the main engine cracked a piston head and we stopped at sea to fit the spare. The ship rolling when lifting or lowering a two-ton piston assembly in the confines of the engine room made things more difficult than usual. The engineers and the donkeymen worked well and by eight o'clock in the morning, tired, lathered in sweat and dirty we were under way again.

Satan was sound asleep in the duty mess when we came out of the engine room and had been there most of the night.

We looked at him in disgust but no one said anything. It had all been said before and had achieved nothing.

Our joints were sore, our muscles were aching and we were lathered in sweat. 'I've got half-a-dozen beers in my fridge. Let's have a beer before we get scrubbed up.'

I left the lads sitting on the hatch to cool off in the morning breeze and went to my cabin to pick up the cold beers. Beer at eight o'clock in the morning is disgusting but so is acute fatigue, stiff joints and work clothes soaked in sweat.

There is one hard and fast rule I insist on. Engine room shoes are removed before entering the accommodation. They can be carried by hand, left in top of the engine room or out on deck, but under no circumstances can they be worn in the ship's accommodation. The accommodation is our living quarters and nothing destroys carpets more than sets of footprints from oil-soaked shoes.

On my return, Satan had come in from the duty mess and was walking through the main saloon with his engine room shoes still on. I could see every one of his oily footprints.

'HEY!' I roared, pointing at the marks he'd made on the saloon carpet.

He made a face at me, gave me a vigorous two-fingered salute and meant to carry on his way.

I'm human. As a human being I have a breaking point, a point where I can take no more and I reached that point at that moment.

I threw the six-pack at him. Then with one hand I grasped him by the neck and slammed him against the bulkhead of the dining saloon with a crash that was probably heard through most of the accommodation. I closed my grip until I could feel the individual shape of the bones and muscles and I squeezed tighter.

His heels were about six inches clear of the deck and his legs kicked and thrashed out frantically. His nails clawed grooves into the back of the hand that pinned him to the wall and I watched his face turn purple.

There was naked terror in his bulging eyes when he knew he was about to die. No longer was there any derision or contempt.

'Let him go, Bob.' Hughie had heard the banging of Satan's feet on the bulkhead and came to investigate.

'Enough, Bob, let him go!'

He prised my fingers off Satan's neck and I let him fall, staggered out to the deck and tried to sit on the edge of the cargo hatch but I was shaking too much. I slumped to the deck and sat there.

It was a few days before Satan's voice could rise above a squeak. But he'd changed in other ways too. He did as he was told. He had lost his aggressiveness. He worked better, but not because he was afraid, but because he suddenly found that in life, he could be hurt. Throughout his life, no one had ever done more than just reprimand him. No one had ever really hurt him or punished him.

And I had nearly killed him.

Time passed and he gradually became a worthy member of the engine room staff. If he spoke, he would immediately ask us if he was being cheeky. If someone needed a hand, he rushed to help, almost begging to be of assistance. When the mess room teapot became empty and the steward wasn't around, he was the one who immediately hurried to fill it.

This was not done through fear of being hurt again. This was done because he had found out that others could hurt him. He found he was not immune to physical punishment.

When I was leaving the ship at the end of my contract, he pushed off the others to carry my suitcases down to the taxi. Then asked if he could shake my hand. Corny? Yes, it was corny, but not to him. When I think back, it wasn't so corny to me either.

Time passed, and about two years later, on another ship, I was being relieved and going home.

The Second Engineer relieving me had a long look at me. 'So you're Bob Jackman? I often wondered what you looked like. We had a Fifth Engineer last trip, a lad called 'Stetten' who never got tired of telling everybody he was once a Bob Jackman cadet. Aye, he was a damned good lad, actually.'

So, Satan, if you ever read this, I wish you well and I'm glad you grew up and became a man.

But, most of us think your parents should be flogged, preferably, publicly.

LANGUAGE MATTERS

In my earliest days at sea our crews hailed from Calcutta and spoke a type of Hindustani that's quite common round the Indian Coast. When working with an Indian crew in that particular shipping company it was to one's advantage to learn the language.

Imagine, for example, saying to an Indian greaser, 'I want a hammer.'

Your request would be met with, 'Sahib?' accompanied with a display of the greaser's open hands and a bewildered look.

'A hammer!'

'Sahib?' This time the bewildered look would be accompanied with a flicker of a smile at the corners of his mouth.

'HAMMER!' This said, the word would be accompanied with the action of one using the tool in question.

The greaser would then sally off and might return a long time later with either a wooden hatch wedge or a cup of tea.

Consequently I found life was so much easier if I could speak the language.

'Soono, hum martool mungta, ur gildi.' This informed my non co-operative greaser that I wanted a hammer and I wanted it quickly. A fringe benefit was that if you could speak their language you soon had inside knowledge of their way of thinking.

For instance, to them, prayers are all important. As a young Fourth Engineer on watch in the engine room at sea I allowed my two greasers and the donkeyman time to say their prayers while on duty. It only took them about seven minutes, they appreciated it and they knew it was a privilege. Any trouble and they could do their praying somewhere else and in their own time.

A year or so later I was Fourth with an Anglo-Indian Second Engineer. He was born in India somewhere and as comfortable with Hindustani as he was with English. This was in contrast with some of my fellow officers who couldn't speak a word of Hindustani and any knowledge they had of the Queen's English was heavily punctuated with four letter words.

One day this aforementioned Anglo-Indian Second Engineer Officer asked my greaser if he could understand everything I said.

'Yes, Sahib. Sometimes the Fourth Engineer's Hindustani is a little bit home-made, but we can always understand him.'

My 'home-made' Hindustani had much to recommend it though and I found I had no trouble communicating.

Our fluent Anglo-Indian Second Engineer Officer one day mentioned that the Indians had no word for 'gloves'. Gloves, he told me, are unknown in India and therefore there is no such word.

With a smug smile on my face, I stuck my head round the storeroom door and bawled to the Storekeeper, 'Cassab? Hart-eshtocking mungta.'

He brought me a pair of 'hand stockings'. Gloves.

I had many such 'home-made' Hindustani words in my early days on board ship. Who knows? Perhaps some of them even found their way into the Hindustani language?

For instance I once asked the same bi-lingual Anglo-Indian Second Engineer Officer if he knew what a 'char punka, uppa-nichi, hawa our panni garri' was?

He looked at me, puzzled. 'A four fan, upside down, wind and water cart?'

I let him think about it for a while before I informed him I was referring to a Sunderland flying boat. My home made Hindustani was not quite so unpractical – in some ways.

In City Line in the mid-1950s, the Indian crew who were not watch keepers were mainly there to do cleaning and labouring work. Some of them had a working knowledge of English as far as their duties were concerned so I had no reason to speak Hindustani unless I thought it necessary. But in learning their language, I also learned their ways and they respected me for that. I knew when I could push and when I couldn't.

Like the time when the Chief Engineer was going home. He was packed and ready and requested the Second Engineer order the Serang, the Indian engine room boss, to have some men carry his luggage ashore.

The Serang refused. 'No, Sahib. That is steward's job. Not engine room man's job.'

In those far-off days, British shipping companies were tugging their forelocks to the Indian authorities and entreating all staff to be very nice to the Indian crew regardless of what it cost. It was something to do with India gaining its independence about eight years earlier and this new power was trickling down to its minions.

About half an hour later when the Engineers were coming up for lunch we found there was a real ding-dong shouting match with the Chief and Second Engineers on one side and the Serang, Tindal and Cassab on the other.

The Second's fists were clenched and the Chief's face was quite purple at the edges when he suddenly spied me.

'You, Fourth,' he roared, 'you understand these buggers, see if you can get them to carry my bags ashore.'

I paused for a few moments, then bowed my head briefly to the Serang, the Tindal and the Cassab, and placed my hands together the way a child does when saying its prayers.

'Serang, burrasahib ka shamin canera lagger.' This was a formal request that the Chief's luggage is taken ashore.

Immediately all three men picked up the suitcases. 'We be very 'delightful' to take the Chief Engineer luggage shoreside.'

Within minutes, the Chief's luggage was being carefully stowed into the waiting taxi.

There were often many amusing moments in language problems on board ship. In Calcutta, we changed crew and my new cabin steward was young and enthusiastic. Since I was Fourth Engineer on the 8-12 watch, I breakfasted in my cabin at 7.30am.

My new cabin steward appeared at 7.20 with a cup of coffee.

'Good morning, Sahib.'

'Good morning.'

'Your morning eggs, Sahib?'

'Yes?'

'You wish them fried, boiled or disturbed?'

Again, another piece of breakfast humour was provided by Arthur, our vegetarian Second Mate. He was particularly nauseated by those who dined on any foods with saturated fat content so was always first at the breakfast table to avoid the sausage-bacon-and-eggs brigade. His breakfast would consist of fruit juice, corn flakes, coffee and toast and he was perplexed why the steward always took so long to serve him.

He liked corn flakes. 'Corn flakes, burrawallah!'

'Burrawallah' means 'big one,' like a big object. He should have said 'jasti', which means 'plenty', a large quantity. I was quite amused by that poor saloon steward patiently picking the large flakes, one at a time, out of the Kellog's box then watching the irate Second Mate immediately crunch them up on his plate before pouring on the milk. Tensions were eased and table service was improved immensely when I increased his knowledge of Hindustani by that one word.

Again, the mynah bird gets its name from the large amount of droppings that rapidly festoon the perches and the bottom of its cage, much more than any other bird of a similar size. Also it is a renowned talker and can refuse to shut up when it has an audience.

My rank was now Second Engineer Officer, or in Hindustani, Manshla *Mistri* Sahib. Indians often have their private little joke by referring to the Second Engineer Officer as the 'Manshla *Mynah* Sahib' until I quietly corrected them with a smile. I've never had to do it twice.

In Calcutta we changed the crew. There was always a gap of two days between the one leaving and the one joining, for reasons best known to our Head Office.

I had no wish to go ashore so I let all the engineers have a day off while I kept an eye on all things of a technical nature on board. It was late in the afternoon when having a look to check all was well with the engine room and the boilers, the telephone rang.

'Second! Come up quick!' The Chief's voice sounded two octaves higher than usual.

His eyes were quite wild when he met me in the alleyway outside his cabin.

'I need you to translate,' he panted as if out of breath. 'There was an Indian bloke came to my door with three young girls. I thought he may be someone important from the shipping office ashore and the three girls were part of his family so I took them in and sat them down. But he doesn't speak much English and I don't speak their damned lingo and it took me a while to work out that he was our next engine room 'Serang' and he was making me a gift of one of the girls for the night!'

I tried hard not to laugh. 'Yes, Chief, calm down.'

'OK, I'm calm. Honestly, I'm calm.' He took a few deep breaths. 'Anyway, I ushered him and his girls out of my cabin as quickly as I could and saw them off down the gangway.'

'So, if they've gone, what do you want me to translate?'

'You've got to translate for me, for Gawd's sake, Bob. He came back! He is here in my cabin now and this time he's brought three small boys! I feel sick!'

In later years I joined a Hong Kong company. Generally, the senior officers consisted of five or six Europeans and all other ranks were Hong Kong Chinese. While I learned to speak quite good Hindustani in a few months, I never managed to learn more than ten words of Chinese in fourteen years. On most occasions, I sailed with Chinese engineers, electricians and crew who could speak quite good English.

One particular young Electrician I had was well educated. 'Why don't you learn to speak Chinese?' he asked me.

I laughed. 'Chinese? It would take five years for me to learn Chinese.'

'What age would you be in five years?'

'In five years I will be thirty-five years old.'

'I see. And what age will you be in five years if you don't learn to speak Chinese?'

As I said, I learned quite a lot from our Chinese Electrician.

I'd been on one particular Hong Kong ship for about twelve months when the new Chief Engineer joined. On his second day on board he wanted to alter his office desk and the light above it.

'I want to put the light further over and make the desk lower. If you give me one of the Chinese I'll do the job myself but I'll need someone to run for tools for me. Give me one of the squad who can speak English.'

'OK, Chief, no problem.'

I left him but as I approached the engine room door I realised there was a problem. Senior Third? Junior Third? Senior Fourth? Junior Fourth? Electrician? Any of the fitters?

I turned back to the Chief's cabin. 'Hey, Chief. None of them speak a word of English!'

I had worked a whole year with that engine room squad and it was just one of the little things about them I hadn't noticed.

A slight deviation from the topic of language involved our Fifth Engineer called 'Paddy' and a group of elderly lady passengers. The bold Paddy was born and reared in the back streets of Belfast, apprenticed in the shipyards and a devout Catholic.

'There's a leak in a pipe in one of the passenger's bathrooms, Bob,' the Chief informed me. 'See what can be done about it.'

So Paddy and I removed the side panel off the bath and took turns of wriggling and squeezing round the end of the bath to see the leak.

'I *** see it!' Paddy gasped. 'It's a right ***.'

'For Heaven's sake, Paddy! Mind your language and keep your voice down. Remember there are loads of old women passengers in these cabins that can hear every word you say.'

'Aye, sorry, Second, really sorry. OK. I promise I'll keep my voice down.'

'And watch your language?'

'Not a swear word will pass my bliddy lips. And that's a promise, Second,' he whispered.

We returned to discussing the job in hand, with Paddy speaking slowly and quietly.

'It's a wee pin hole on a bend in the cold water pipe away underneath. I can just reach it if I wriggle in far enough. I will use the paraffin blowlamp and put a wee dab of soft solder on it. That should do it.'

I appreciated the effort he was making to talk quietly and without using foul language. But it didn't last.

I was on the bottom plates in the engine room ten minutes later when the Chief was on the phone. 'For Gawd's sake Bob, get that mad Irish Fiver out of the passengers' accommodation. All the old women are up in the Captain's cabin and they're in hysterics, screaming their heads off! Get him out of there,' he roared.

It took about one minute and eight seconds for me to travel from the bottom of the engine room to the passenger's bathroom and Paddy, five decks up.

'Right, Paddy, you clown, you promised you wouldn't swear or shout. You've just frightened the living daylights out of all the women passengers. There's a hysterical bunch of them in the Captain's cabin now, screaming their heads off. So tell me about it.'

'Honest, Second, it couldn't have been me! I certainly didn't swear – not one single swear word, honest! I'll just tell you what happened. I had managed to wriggle in to a position round the end of the bath to reach the leak and the greaser handed me any tools I needed. I used the blowlamp, soldered the pipe and passed it out with the rest of the tools to the greaser. As I wriggled out, my backside pushed against the flame of the blowlamp and it burnt my bum. It made me jump, but all I did was look at the greaser and tell him nicely that he should not have put the blowlamp in my way. Honestly, Second, that was what happened.'

There are times in situations like this when you just don't know what to believe. This wasn't one of them.

THE PUNISHMENT SHIP

In my forty-odd years at sea I've sailed with a wide variety of Chief Engineers. Some of them were gentlemen I'd give a month's pay to sail with again and my life has been made richer just by knowing them. Chief Engineers like 'Mac' Dryden, Kevin O'Mahoney, Jim Weir, Bill Anderson, Joe Cochran, Bob Graham and dozens more that slip my ageing mind.

But there were others, like the 'Pig'.

I had been on eighteen-month trips with a British company sailing out of Hong Kong, then came home and married the girl who had waited for me so patiently. When a lovely house came on the market in our village, we made the down payment, took on a mortgage and left ourselves quite low on ready finances. All this happened within five weeks in 1962.

One well-known British company which shall remain nameless, advertised for a Certificated Second Engineer Officer for a three month trip straight down the West African coast and home again. I knew if I took it, it would allow me to be back by Christmas so I applied and got the job.

That was when I met 'The Pig'. He waddled, carrying his great pot belly in front of him and was mentally as thick as two short planks.

'I'll take you round the engine room and show you what's what.'

'Aye, Chief, but where's the Second?'

'He left, he wasn't much good, have you been with opposed piston Harland and Wolff's before? I don't suppose you have. This one smokes a bit, but it's OK really.'

He waddled away like a ruptured duck before I could say anything and my guided tour of the engine room began. It wasn't that bad and I'd taken over much worse.

A rather surly forty-year old in a boiler suit was leaning against the main engine controls when we arrived at the bottom plates.

The Chief led me over to meet him. 'This is the Third Engineer.'

I put out my hand to shake his and he ignored it. His eyes drifted from the Chief to me then back again before he contemptuously turned his back on us.

'That's what they gave me for a Third.' The Chief leaned forward and spoke louder. 'And he's bloody useless.'

The Fourth Engineer was a hyperactive four-foot-six-inch boy that hurried everywhere with great big strides. He saw us, but wouldn't come near.

The Chief pointed him out to me as he scampered round the end of the main engine.

'This is his last chance before he gets the boot from the company,' the Chief smirked. 'Oh, and watch the Electrician. He gets violent if he's been drinking. He's getting kicked out as well.'

The rest of the engine room staff consisted of two bewildered young boys from a training school of sorts and a junior engineer straight from a garage in Belfast.

When the Chief and I came back up into the accommodation we parted company at my cabin door. Before he left, he turned and pushed his finger to an inch from my nose and squinted along it as if it was a gun barrel.

'One more thing, Second Engineer what-ever-your-name-is, I give the orders around here, and you better learn that fast.' Then he ambled off to his cabin and closed the door.

What in Hell had I joined? This was a *British* Company?

There is an old adage in the Merchant Navy that a Second Engineer is either a bad bastard or a stupid bastard and the choice is his and his alone.

When I had been doing the grand tour with the Chief, I was still dressed in a clean shirt and a pair of slacks. I changed into a boiler suit and set off 'down below' again. The Third was still standing by the main engine controls and again he turned his back on me when he saw me coming.

My hand shot up between his legs, grabbed his wedding tackle, lifted his feet clear of the deck and squeezed hard. I found he was not the strong silent type after all. In fact, he wasn't strong and he squealed high notes an operatic soprano would have been justly proud of.

A few moments passed before I released my grip and he backed off rapidly, holding himself very tenderly with two hands.

I smiled at him. 'Let's you and I not get off to a bad start, Third. You and I understand each other now. OK?'

He seemed to have lost a lot of his bravado.

I left him and wandered off to have my own personal tour round the job before returning to my cabin to look over the usual Second Engineer's paperwork. There was no engine room work book, record book, repair list, stores list or spare gear list. There was no list of stores or spares that had been received while we were in Liverpool.

Basically, I wasn't too bothered. My suitcases were still unpacked, I hadn't 'signed on,' and there was nothing stopping me from turning round and going straight home again. The ship was due to sail in twenty-four hours. I felt like leaving anyway, so what had I to lose?

I walked into the Chief's cabin without knocking and sat down.

We had words. We had lots of words, but in the end, I was given the previous Second Engineer's workbook and all the other books pertaining to the engine room maintenance.

The 'Pig' knew I was on the verge of walking off and he'd have lots of explaining to do at the Head Office if I did. No doubt my predecessor said a lot to the hierarchy when he left and none of it would be very flattering.

When I met the Captain he quietly informed me that no one would sail with the 'Pig' except those who had no option, like the Third, the Fourth and the Electrician. The Junior Engineer and the two cadets had never been to sea before so they didn't know what to expect.

A 'punishment ship' is so called because if you don't change your ways you are out of the company. None of their company's Second Engineers would sail with him and so they were forced to advertise.

We left Liverpool and headed for West Africa.

On sea watches, the Fourth had one cadet, the Third had the other cadet and I took Paddy, the Junior Engineer from Belfast. I had to take Paddy because his Irish accent was so thick I was the only one who knew what he was saying. Actually, Paddy was the best man I had out of all of them and it was his first trip to sea.

Being 4-8 watch, I was having the necessary two hours sleep before going on watch at four o'clock. I had just dropped off when there was a sudden rapid heavy banging from the engine room. It felt like World War Three had just started and we were heavily involved. I was running before my feet hit the deck and I slid my way down to the engine room using handrails only.

'Knock that generator off!' I roared at the Third.

He screamed back at me. 'The Pig wants it on. It always sounds like that!'

I reached up and shut the throttle and let the generator clatter to a halt.

Immediately, the engine room phone rang and again the Pig and I had words. We had lots of words. But in the end he agreed to let me check the generator over when I took over my watch and slammed the phone down. I could feel him gnashing his teeth with rage, five decks above me.

So, to make a long story longer, when Paddy and I took over our watch, we started work on that diesel generator immediately. For the technically minded, we found that when No 1 piston was on top dead centre, the inlet or induction valve was still closed. It should have opened about ten degrees at least, before top dead centre. If No 1 is out, all six cylinders are out. This is elementary engineering knowledge. This is primary school stuff.

Between us, we removed the end casing and shifted the timing chain two links, bringing the camshaft timing a lot nearer to what it should be. Then we put back the end cover and started her up. There are few sounds as sweet to the ear of an engineer as the sound of a well-tuned diesel.

'Is she just not wonderful, Second, just wonderful?' Paddy's young face beamed at me.

So, the watch came to an end with No 2 generator purring contentedly. The logbook was made up, Fourth and his cadet took over the watch and Paddy and I headed for the showers. When we were dressed we headed to the smoke room for a beer or six.

The Pig was waiting for us in the Officers smoke room, standing alone and drumming his fingers on the bar. Fellow officers, Captain and Chief Officer included, were quietly seated around, waiting for the fireworks. Chief Steward was playing bartender. I felt like Gary Cooper in 'High Noon.'

'Two beers, please.'

We were served two beers.

Absolute silence in the room.

Then the Pig cleared his throat. 'Now then, Mister Second Engineer, you better listen to me, and listen good. I said I wanted No2 Generator on and the Third Engineer put it on. You ordered the Third to stop it because it was noisy.'

I took a sip of beer and nodded. 'Yes, Chief.'

He raised his voice to ensure everyone heard. 'You countermanded my order. Well, it just so happens, Mister Second Engineer, there is nothing wrong with that generator. The fault lies with the ship's hull and there's nothing can be done about it. These bottles and glasses in this bar rattle like mad when that generator is on, but it cannot be helped. I repeat, the fault lies with the hull design. I am satisfied with it, the company are satisfied with it and so were the Chiefs before me.'

He paused to let the full weight of his words be heard by all then walked round me to the smokeroom telephone.

'Now if you don't mind, Mister Second Engineer, I'll just tell the Fourth to start No 2 generator and you'll just have to learn to put up with the almighty rattling of bottles and glasses, just like the rest of us.'

Paddy and I looked at each other. He was quivering, tensed, waiting for this moment.

'Chief?' I raised my eyebrows; I had the look of an innocent. Now it was my turn to speak so that everyone could hear me quite clearly. 'No 2 generator is on. No2 generator is running now, very sweetly. We can hardly hear it. Can anyone hear it? No bottles rattling, no glasses rattling anywhere. It was just a simple thing. Its camshaft timing was about ten degrees out and Paddy and I just put it right. It was easy.'

There was a long silence then someone giggled. The Chief put down the phone, cleared his throat and looked at all the faces that were struggling to hide their laughter. After a few minutes he coughed, cleared his throat and spoke.

'Did anyone hear how West Ham got on today?'

Everyone burst into laughter and he left the smoke room with his head down and taking his beer with him.

So the voyage continued. The Third lost some of his aggressiveness but he'd never be an engineer, the Fourth had regular tantrums and would burst into tears if things didn't go right for him. The two cadets were still just bewildered schoolboys. The Electrician overhauled the electric winches and we all stayed well out of his way.

Only Paddy was of any use in the engine room. He could use tools and he was eager to learn engineering.

Another endearing habit of the Pig was his love of the telephone. In port, the two cadets and Paddy were on alternate weeks on night duty. He'd call them at various times during the night to give them jobs to do then phone them at ten-minute intervals to ask if they had done them.

There was nothing wrong with that engine room that an ordinary squad of marine engineers couldn't put right in a short time.

We returned to Liverpool five months later. The cadets' parents met them as we docked and took them home, the Third and Fourth Engineers were suddenly no longer on board and no one had seen them go. The Electrician had disappeared and only Paddy and I were left on board.

Both of us had been on our feet all day and there was no one to take over the night duty in the engine room from ten o'clock that evening. We'd all been 'paid off' on arrival and were not due to be signed on again until the next day.

Paddy appeared at my cabin door. 'I take it there's been nobody turned up then, Second? No one at all, at all?'

'No one, Paddy. We'll have to split the night watch between us.'

He paused.

'Well, if it's OK with you, Second, I'll do all night on my own and if I feel I'm getting too sleepy, I promise I'll call you. But there is one thing.'

'What's that?'

'Will you tell the Pig not to keep phoning me when I'm down below? Please, Second?'

So, that was the arrangement we agreed on. Paddy went to put on his boiler suit and I went to have words with the Pig.

'Now you listen, and listen carefully.' This time it was *my* finger that was an inch from *his* nose. 'The junior has had two hours sleep since four o'clock this morning and now he's going to do an all-night watch. Now keep your stupid hands off that telephone. Do you understand me? Do not keep phoning him during the night! LEAVE HIM ALONE!' I stormed.

'Yes, OK, OK. I'll leave him alone.'

'You won't phone him?'

'I won't phone him.'

I left him sitting at his desk, told Paddy he had promised not to phone him and made my way back to my cabin to sleep.

I was wakened by my cabin door being thrown open.

'Right, Second, I'm going home! I'm going home! That Pig kept phoning me all night. All night, driving me mad! I'm going home! I've had enough! Here, I've brought you a cup of tea! It's six-thirty. I'm going HOME!' He was shaking with rage.

I swung my legs out of the bunk and yawned. 'Do something for me, Paddy?'

'Of course, to be sure I will, anything. For you, anything!'

'Let me drink my tea. I think I'll go home as well.'

Within minutes, I was packed and ready for shoreside. I walked into the Pig's cabin and shook him awake roughly.

'You stupid clown! You bliddy idiot! You kept telephoning the engine room and had that boy running around like a madman all night. Well, Pig, I hope you know how to start generators and put them on the switchboard for they'll start cargo at eight o'clock.'

'The Third...?'

'Gone, so is the Fourth. And Paddy, the young lad you had running around all night is leaving now. And, Pig, so am I.'

I slammed his cabin door with a bang and Paddy and I picked up our cases and set out for the railway station.

We had to wait for our trains so we had a couple of cups of British Rail coffee in the Liverpool station buffet to pass the time.

'Paddy, you were made for the Merchant Navy. Don't quit! You're a damn good lad and I'm proud to have sailed with you.'

Paddy was a good lad. If only there were more like him.

'MAC'

Mac was one of the finest Chief Engineers I ever sailed with.

In our early days together, we were in his cabin having a nightcap when he was in a talking mood. I learned he was a 'Geordie' born and bred, reared in the back streets of Newcastle yet quiet and well mannered and with a great knowledge of the finer arts. He could quote Oscar Wilde, Voltaire and pieces from Shakespeare's lesser known plays. A mere five foot eight in height and though twenty years my senior he was as lean and as fit as any Olympic runner. It was only on the rarest occasions when he was outraged at something or somebody that he lapsed into broad Geordie and then he was not a man to be trifled with.

As the months went passed our friendship grew. If he had a fault, it was his overwhelming love of ladies and he had his merry way with so many in every port we visited. I must admit, though, that he was always very selective.

'Mac? Don't you ever think you may catch something? I mean, I know you would be careful, but....?' I left the sentence unfinished.

He eased himself out of his armchair, crossed the cabin to his drinks cupboard and opened it wide.

'See that, Bob? Well stocked with whisky, rum, vodka, gin and sherry for the ladies. There are also a few good wines behind them. But you see that one bottle of gin with a slightly torn label. I keep it to one side. That's the one you never touch. If ever you are stuck for a bottle, help yourself, take what you like, but never that one.

His finger was pointed at me for emphasis.

'Okay, Mac, why? Why not that one?'

He closed the cupboard doors and returned to his beer. 'After I've had a woman, I come back on board, pour myself a large glass of gin from that bottle and soak my willie in it for a few minutes.'

I had to laugh. 'You have a large glass of gin every time you've had a woman? Holy mackerel! That would add to the night's expenses.'

He shook his head. 'No, not really.' Then he smiled the smile of the innocent. 'I just pour the gin back into the bottle and keep it for Lloyd's Surveyors, Marine Superintendents and other characters of an unsavoury nature. I've carried that bottle around with me for a long time. Years, in fact.'

And Mac certainly loved the ladies. They were not just sexual conquests. He truly *loved* them.

Like the time in Sasebo in Japan when this big hulking brute of an American sailor started getting really nasty with the little old Mama-san in the Acey-Deucy Bar.

Mac quietly rose to his feet and walked over to confront the Yank. 'Sorry, mister,' he smiled pleasantly. 'I'm asking you to calm down and not cause any unpleasantness. This is a nice bar and we tend to keep it that way. Okay?'

The Yank blinked at him, stretched to his full height and clenched his fists. 'Yeah? And who in the Hell are you, buster?'

'They call me 'Mac' and I'm the bouncer for all the bars down this side of the street as far as 'The Bamboo Cat.' My friend, Yukio Tani, does the other side of the street as far as 'The Hollywood'. Mac's smile widened and he poked the Yank hard on the chest with his index finger, 'So, I'm just telling you that it's a forty minute run in an ambulance to get you from here to a hospital bed and I'm quite capable of putting you into a hospital bed for a while. Do you want to chance it?'

There was a deathly silence except for the juke box playing Nat King Cole's 'Mona Lisa.' A chair scraped as it was moved away from a table. Somebody coughed.

Suddenly the big Yank backed off and left. Mac returned to our table.

I looked at him in amazement. 'Wow! Are you a Judoka?'

He smiled. 'No, I am not a Judoka. In fact I'm not a fighting man of any kind.'

'What would you have done if he'd hit you, Chief?'

'Don't really know, actually,' he answered thoughtfully then smiled. 'I would probably have had a month in a hospital bed somewhere.'

It just wasn't in the man to allow an elderly woman he'd never met before, to be abused by a savage brute like that American sailor. As I said, Mac truly loved all women.

Or again, in Novorosisk in Russia, we came out of the Officers' Club when the ground was covered with a layer of snow and the air temperature was dropping rapidly. An old beggar woman wrapped in rags was trying to sell a tiny bunch of wild flowers to anyone passing. We had spent all our roubles and our taxi was with the complements of the Port Authorities to ensure we returned to our ship. Mac turned to her, took her wild flowers and gave her his watch.

It just wasn't in the man to allow a woman he'd never met before be bullied by a big American sailor. Neither was he capable of ignoring the plight of a frail old woman begging on a freezing night in Novorosisk.

'What was your last Company, Mac? I mean, what brought you to sailing on Hong Kong tramps?'

'My last company was Athel Line but like most British companies, the gentlemen polishing their backsides at office desks didn't know the first thing about ships. Would you believe that the twit in charge of personnel didn't know that Engineers were officers? Or that in some companies the Chief Engineer is much higher paid than the Captain? They held up one of the ships once because they couldn't get a Second Mate. The Third Mate had a Second Mate's ticket, so why not move him up and let the Captain do the Third Mate's watch? We could do twelve knots, a mere fourteen miles per hour, in a great big empty ocean and yet we were held up in port for eight days because we didn't have a Second Mate.'

He sprang out of his chair and looked out his cabin window with his back to me. Then he took a deep breath and sighed.

'Bob, we have the biggest Merchant Navy the world has ever seen. Bureaucracy and ignorance will destroy it.' He picked up the whisky bottle and surveyed its contents. 'There's enough for a small one each.' He poured and the empty bottle was placed in his wastepaper basket.

'So then, did you leave because of this business with the Second Mate?'

'No, I left because of a Second Engineer.' He looked at my puzzled expression, and went on. 'I was informed by the office that my next Second Engineer Officer was not certificated. I would have to accept, what they were obliged to call, 'a permit Second Engineer' and I objected most strongly. I asked them if the Captain would sail with an uncertificated First Mate and they were stunned that I could even suggest such a thing. Well, I told them if there wasn't a proper qualified Second Engineer on board on sailing day, I would leave.'

He swilled the remains of his Scotch round the bottom of his glass and smacked his lips.

'And did you?' I prompted.

He nodded, a smile touching the corners of his mouth. 'Two hours before sailing I had my bags packed and was ready to leave. Four top brass including the personnel twit walked into my cabin. They wheedled, threatened, pleaded and raged for an hour, but I remained pleasant and still refused to sail. And, of course, if I left, the ship couldn't sail.' Mac swirled the last of his whisky round his glass and drank it. 'They blacklisted me. No British company would take me, so I quite happily joined this Hong Kong Company. I've never regretted it for one single moment.'

'No unpleasant memories, Mac?'

'No unpleasant memories. But one particularly happy memory, Bob, concerning that little group from Head Office.' He smiled over the top of his glass. 'When I walked out of my cabin, the four from Head Office were still sitting there, drinking gin and tonics, working their way through my bottle of gin. You know the gin bottle I am referring to: The one with the torn label.'

THE GIBRALTAR GIRL

H arry came from a place called 'Gilliman's Creek,' a remote watering hole in the Australian outback where girls were as rare as two-headed unicorns. He stood well over six-foot in his stocking soles, as lean and as fit as a three-year-old greyhound and good-looking enough for a career in Hollywood. However, this fine upstanding gentleman had one fault; he was hopeless in the company of ladies. He had run off to sea as a sixteen-year-old and knew his way round bars and bar girls but when he was in the close proximity of true ladies he fell apart. He was also one of the best Chief Engineers and one of the nicest guys I ever had the pleasure to sail with.

Our happy ship had a complement of four Europeans, one Australian (Harry) and about twenty plus Hong Kong Chinese when we pulled into Gibraltar that summer.

'Right, Chief, all set for shoreside tonight! All set to sample the local brew?'

'Not tonight, Bob. I've got paperwork and a couple of letters to write. Stuff I should have sent from the last port. But, tomorrow, I'll be ready and I'll be there, fair dinkum.'

So Captain Mel Hooper, the Mate Bill Court, Bobo the Sparks and I headed shoreside to see what the

Gibraltar bars and the nightlife had to offer. I remember that bar we went to in a quiet part of the town. It was quiet, lavishly furnished and the kind of place where you felt you could entertain the wife of a Baptist minister.

People ashore always picture seafarers as a breed that go into low dives, get drunk and go to bed with prostitutes. The reality is often quite different. A meal in a five star restaurant with a bottle of good wine, Irish coffee to follow, then a theatre or cinema show and a taxi back to the ship is often much nearer the truth. We envy the local youngsters with pretty young ladies on their arms, but it takes time to become acquainted with pretty young ladies and seamen in the world's ports don't have time to become acquainted.

The waitress that came to our table had a nice smile and a notebook.

'Four pints of your best brew, please,' whispered Captain Hooper in confidential tones.

'I'm sorry, sir,' she whispered back, 'we don't serve pints. Will glasses do?' It was just that kind of place.

It felt great just being off the ship for a while, to absorb different surroundings, to see different people, to drink different beers, to have a bit of space that was quiet and restful.

It was while our waitress was serving the beers that we saw a very lovely woman appear behind the bar and talk with the barmaid. She had a pure angelic look that made Merchant Navy seafarers' breathing difficult and raised their blood pressures sky high.

'Who is the tall girl behind the bar? The manageress?'

The waitress cast a quick look and smiled at us. 'That's Helen, Helen Douglas Ferris. She owns the bar. And, isn't it a funny thing, but all the male customers want to know who she is?'

So we drooled at a distance, watched every thing she did and talked about football. We watched her move to welcome customers and our pulses gathered speed when she approached our table.

'Is everything to your satisfaction, gentlemen?'

I saw three shining faces beam at her and heard three voices gushing to tell her how everything was so wonderful. I smiled politely, briefly, and hid a yawn that she noticed.

When she left to welcome others, the subject half-heartedly returned to football and she returned to the bar.

'I think I would like a cigar.'

I made my way there too and surveyed the selection of cigars behind the bar without paying much attention to her other than to be polite. I bought a packet of five and as I paid for them I looked at her innocently.

'Excuse me, but did you have something stuck to your hand when you came to our table a few minutes ago?'

'Something stuck to my hand?' She held out both her hands for me to see there was nothing in them. I took them in mine and studied the lines on her palms for a couple of moments then gave her a worried look.

I smiled. 'Sorry. I thought I saw something. Piece of sticky paper or something.' Then shook my head and turned to walk back to our table.

'You read my hands! You saw something in my hands.'

I smiled at her, again shook my head and returned to the others.

Sparky was curious. 'What was all that about?'

I took a cigar out of the packet and lit it. 'Cigars. Tell me more about Arsenal beating West Ham.'

I knew she was watching me but I never once looked her way. I laughed and joked with the others, asked some questions about football, had a few more beers then came the time to call it a night. She intercepted me at the door while the others were leaving.

'You read my hands. You *saw* something in my hands.'

I made her wait as if deciding whether or not to say anything. Then I nodded.

'Please tell me,' she said softly. Her closeness was making my heart play 'woops-a-daisy' and I fought to remain calm.

While my compatriots had been discussing goals and penalties my brain had been in overdrive and my thoughts had not been on football.

I hesitated.

'Please?'

'Are you sure?'

She nodded.

Then I sighed as if succumbing to her wishes. 'I saw a very tall man. Very tall. I saw pain and fire, but I also saw true love: A very sweet and powerful love. I don't know what it means. I can only tell you what I saw.'

'Can you say when?'

'I don't know. I have no way of knowing. There is no time scale in what the hands say.' I stepped away from her. 'Fire and pain and love. I told you I didn't want to tell you. I'm sorry. I must go.'

Once back on board I barged into Harry's cabin and dragged him out of the book he was reading.

'WAKEY! WAKEY! There's a gorgeous angel ashore and she's dying to meet you. Harry! Chief! She's truly an angel, not only a beautiful lady but a beautiful person as well. It's a posh bar called 'The Gainsborough Lady', a lovely place. Another thing – you're on your own – and, Harry, she loves you madly.'

I left a bewildered Harry sitting up in bed, then I closed the cabin door and immediately opened it again. 'And don't forget to take a full box of matches with you!'

Well, it happened. The following night he sat at the bar with a beer, a cigarette, an evening paper and she was there. Two large Scotches later, under the pretence of lighting a cigarette, he developed enough courage to make his whole box of matches flare up and burn the tips of his fingers more seriously than he intended. But everything went better than I had planned. She was looking the other way when the matches flared up.

He plunged his fingers into the small jug of water on the counter and succeeded in knocking it over on to his lap. He stood aghast and surveyed his wet trousers.

'I'm terribly, terribly sorry,' he stammered, 'I feel such a fool.'

She turned her head and laughed, then held up the flap in the bar. 'You'd better come through.'

He followed her into the small storeroom behind the bar and stood back as she switched on an electric wall fire.

'Stand close to it. You'll soon dry off.'

'You're very kind,' he muttered but she'd already left to return a minute later with a large bartender's apron and a towel.

'Take your trousers off, dry yourself with the towel and put on the apron to guard your modesty. I'll be back in a minute.' She smiled at him. 'And don't panic, I'll knock on the door before I come in.'

The minutes passed and door received a knock. He had dried himself, changed into the bartender's apron and was holding his trousers and underpants before the heater.

'Everything all right?' She sat on the edge of a table, smiling at him, and letting her legs swing to and fro.

'Well, I do feel a proper twit.'

'What happened? How did you manage to knock over the water jug, anyway?'

'I was lighting a cigarette and the whole box of matches flared up and burnt my fingers. I stuck my hand into the water jug and knocked it on to my lap.'

The smile left her face, her eyes widened and she stopped swinging her legs.

Harry looked at her. 'Did I say something wrong?'

She slid off the table, took his hands in hers and examined his reddened fingertips. Now she was the one who became excited and flustered.

'I'll find some cream or something for the burns.' She muttered as she went quickly out the door.

When she returned, Harry had changed back into his underpants and trousers and left the neatly folded bartender's apron on the table.

She produced a soothing cream of sorts and some bandages and dressed his injured fingers, while keeping her eyes away from his. The top of her head was level with his chin.

'Look at me,' he whispered, trembling. Her eyes looked into his, searching, then she pulled his face down to hers and they kissed.

Two days later we sailed for Capetown and other African ports then Harry's contract ended when we crossed the Indian Ocean to Mauritius. During the voyage he had become terribly pre-occupied with his own thoughts. After Mauritius he paid off and I never saw him again.

But two years later, on another ship with other acquaintances, we were talking about whom we knew, who we had sailed with and what ships we had been on. I mentioned Harry.

'Harry, Chief Engineer?' The Chief Electrician spoke as he lit his pipe. 'Tall Australian chap? Yes, Harry was a real gentleman. Yes, he married a girl in Gibraltar. A lovely couple.'

I said nothing, but the thought did cross my mind that perhaps I should give up the sea and start a business telling people's fortunes. Where could I buy a nice crystal ball?

'Yeah, Harry brought her with him last trip. She's a fully qualified midwife, you know. Quite plain looking...'

'Quite plain looking?' I gaped at the Chief Lecky in surprise. 'She was one beautiful creature! It was me who arranged their first date. She was gorgeous! She had a pub right in the centre of Gibraltar. 'The Gainsborough Lady' it's called. She owned it.'

'That's right.' Lecky waved the stem of his pipe at me. 'That's right enough. But that one threw herself at Harry and ended up pregnant after a two-day fling with him. He went back about nine months later but she didn't want to know him.'

'So what happened then?'

'He married the midwife.'

AH MAH, THE COOK

Though he had two young galley boys to assist him, old Ah Mah did most of the work himself. He was often found late at night, cleaning under the oil-fired galley stoves, washing behind cupboards or checking the foodstuffs for the next day's menus. The ship's galley was his domain and he kept it super clean.

The burners on the galley stove were of a type that performed well when serviced every week, a routine job I usually allotted to our youngest junior engineer. This was for two reasons; the first reason being that he had to learn to adapt to the routine of others without causing friction and the second reason being that it gave him a touch of responsibility.

'The cook is the boss of the galley,' I told him. 'Never enter his galley without acknowledging him. You can ignore every other blighter you find in the galley but never the cook and this little old man is damned good at his job. He has earned respect. And another thing: Make sure you leave the place as clean as you found it.'

So Junior Engineer Officer Sammy and I picked up some tools from the engine room and made our way to the galley.

'Good morning, Chief Cook, everything OK?'

The frail little figure nodded, his face all happy smiles. 'All velly good. Number one, two, four stove cold, number three maybe little bit hot. All OK, maybe?'

I laid my hand briefly on number three stove. 'Yes, it's OK. Not too hot.'

I stood by the junior for a few minutes while he set to work on the burners but he seemed to know what he was doing. I turned my attention to the rest of the equipment in the galley.

'Everything working OK, Chief Cook?'

His smiling face suddenly collapsed to a picture of abject misery and his head fell on to his chest. 'A bad man steal my beer.'

'Someone steal your beer? Tell me about it, Chief Cook.'

He went to the cabinet refrigerator, opened the door and pointed to a can of Carew's Black Stout on the shelf.

'My beer. Carew's Black Stout. Every morning I put one beer here. All time some bad man steal.'

I gave this a few moments thought and took his can of beer from the refrigerator. Using the junior's screwdriver I pierced two small holes in the bottom of the can. Picking up a mug, I dribbled half of the Black Stout into it and gave it to the cook.

'You drink this. I come back maybe fifteen minutes. You see junior engineer do good job. OK?'

Brian St John Early was Second Mate and like all off-duty Second Mates, he had his feet on the desk, a book on his lap and a beer in his hand. The keys to the medical locker dangled from a nail by his desk.

'You want a cupful of Black Draught! A whole cupful, Bob? Who for? Ten bunged-up engine room donkeymen? Is there an epidemic of constipated seafarers on board I don't know about?'

'To catch a thief.'

He contemplated this for a whole ten seconds, said 'Ah!' closed his book, downed his beer, swung his feet off his desk, reached for his keys and stood up.

'One cupful of Black Draught coming up!'

At the medical locker, Brian held the can while I used a pipette to transfer a cupful of the deadly Black Draught into the can of Black Stout. It took time, but it was a labour of love. When the can was full, two tiny dabs of soft solder sealed it again.

I returned to the galley and the Chief Cook.

'You see this one?' I asked, holding up the can. 'This one half beer, half Black Draught. You savvy Black Draught?'

His eyes widened in wonder as he looked at me before slowly turning his gaze to the can in my hand.

'Black Draught inside?'

'You savvy this Black Draught?'

'Me savvy! So?'

To convince me he was well acquainted with the powerful effect one spoonful of Black Draught could have on one's bowels, he immediately squatted on the galley deck, shut his eyes tight, squeezed his nostrils shut with one hand and rapidly flapped the other behind his rear end. His portrayal of the effects that a spoonful of Black Draught could have on the human body was disgusting but accurate.

'Yes, quite.'

The can with its deadly purgative was gently placed back to its original place in the cabinet refrigerator. But whether the thief twigged there was something suspicious about that can of beer or not, I don't know.

Weeks went passed and it was never stolen. But with Ah Mah, I had gained a friend for life.

We sailed to New York, Philadelphia and Baltimore. It was in Baltimore about 8.30pm on a Sunday when the quartermaster on gangway duty knocked on my cabin door.

'There's a tanker lorry with three ton of lub oil for you, Second. What shall I tell him?'

'It's OK, I'll talk to him.'

There's often some kind of racket goes on where goods are delivered to the ship by drivers who claim overtime for working unsociable hours. I suspect they sleep all day.

This big fellow had a beer belly, a three-day growth on his chin and the lower half of his fat face slowly worked on a wad of gum.

'I gotcha cylinder lub oil.'

'Sorry, mister, there's no one on board to take your oil. Just bring it back in the morning.'

'Supposing I don't wanna bring it back in the morning?' He took a step towards me. His voice was low and menacing.

'Then don't.' I smiled, turned towards the accommodation, stopped at the entrance door and looked back at him.

'Anything else, mister?'

He spat out the gum, glowered at me and swore silently, then went ashore and climbed into his lorry. The quartermaster and I watched him drive off, the tanker's tyres squealing as he turned at the end of the sheds.

It was nine o'clock in the morning when the hulking brute and his tanker re-appeared. I had Willie, the Fourth Engineer, show him where to connect his hose and left them with it.

We were to take three ton of main engine cylinder lubricating oil and run it down into an empty four ton tank. The Fourth was left in charge and I went off to attend to matters elsewhere, confident that nothing could go wrong. How could anything go wrong? Running three ton into an empty four ton tank?

'GUSHER!'

Oil had spewed out of the top of the tank and on to the deck making it as slippery as an Olympic ice rink. How in the Hell could that have happened? Pouring three tons of oil into a four-ton tank and it overflows?

The Chinese engine room crew were mopping it up, gathering it into buckets and saving it any way they could.

Willie appeared. 'I signed for the oil. The tanker driver was in a hurry to be off. He said he'd a long way to go.'

I was watching the level in the tank slowly going down when it dawned on me. After filling the tank, tanker drivers always blow compressed air through their filling hose to empty it. Our tanker driver had been injecting compressed air into the lubricating oil while it was filling, causing it to froth up like a draught beer.

He was probably battering his way down the motorway at top speed by now, laughing all the way to his next job, leaving us with two ton in our tank and less than one ton in buckets.

The Chief was not amused and he and I had much to say to each other. However, thinking back, if I eliminate all the swear words we blasted at each other, neither of us really said very much.

I walked out on deck to cool my rage.

A few minutes passed and a sympathetic Ah Mah appeared behind me with a cold can of Carew's Black Stout.

'Please, Second Engineer, you drink this one.'

I was at the lowest end of an acute depression, but I still managed a smile for the old man.

'This one not mixed with Black Draught, is it, Chief Cook?'

He raised his eyes in innocence. 'No, no, Second Engineer. I give my Black Draught beer to tanker man. He drink it all up and go away velly much quick.'

AN OPPONENT – NOT AN ENEMY

D avy Stewart hailed from Greenock and had played more than a few games for his home team, Greenock Morton, before coming to sea. He still took every opportunity to 'kick a ball around' for them when he went home on leave. As years went by he developed a bone condition that made his bones brittle so his days in any active sport were over. Otherwise Davy, our Chief Officer, was an ordinary bloke who took great care not to break any bones.

Until we arrived in Chingwantao in 1958.

Like me, he was one of the five Europeans sailing with a Hong Kong crew on the frenzied China Coast coal run. This coal run was a nightmare shuttle service from Shanghai to Chingwantao, or Shanghai to Dairen, with coal loaded and discharged at a furious speed by commando dockers. Alongside the berths, loudspeakers constantly blasted out martial music interrupted by rousing battle cries, speeches in Chinese and arc lights that shone dimly through the eternal smog of coal dust. Ship's engineers fought hard battles every hour of the day and night to keep winches and engines in some form of working order. To the Communist Chinese ashore we were branded as a necessary evil because their 'Big Leaps Forward' and their 'Five Year Plans' needed our ships and our expertise. If ships were wrecked in the process, they were left to rot and their crews sent home.

After seven hard months we returned to Hong Kong for repairs, stores and spare parts. We felt stunned. We moved like zombies. All our joints ached. Muscles were as taut as violin strings and the constant roar of the winches hadn't allowed us the luxury of sleep. Consequently our Chinese crew staggered off home and the new Hong Kong Chinese crew joined.

Hong Kong is a paradise. Not just for the bars, the girls, the bright lights, but for the *people*. They are warm and trustworthy; they laugh a lot and it's so easy to make friends.

For a mad forty-eight hours we sampled all that Hong Kong, Kowloon and Wanchai had to offer before returning to the ship and returning to the nightmare of the China Coal Run.

On board ship, when some normality returned, I found I had bought a football. I remembered being in various bars and nightclubs, lugging this football around with me but only vaguely aware of where or why I'd bought it. It probably seemed a good idea at the time.

So back to the bedlam of coal running in the People's Republic of Communist China, but this time, we had a football! The first time we found a few minutes to bounce the ball in the dock area of Chingwantao, armed guards came running. Their rifle butts nudged us all the way back to the ship. We were not allowed to play while those in the Peoples Republic of Communist China worked. Shanghai and Dairen gave us the same harsh treatment.

So the ball was relegated to a cupboard in our duty mess. Sometimes one of us would pick it up, hold it lovingly, talk about football games we'd seen or played, but the ball was always returned to the cupboard. A Chinese steward whispered that our new junior third and senior fourth engineers had both been Hong Kong schoolboy champions in earlier days. Both of them were too shy or too modest to tell us themselves.

Maybe so, but the ball still remained in the mess room cupboard and gradually became forgotten as the nightmare of China's next Five Year Plan rolled on.

A couple of months passed. We arrived in Chingwantao one day about noon, shut down the engines and were preparing to start maintenance work in the stinking hot engine room when the Captain came dashing into our duty mess.

'Believe me or believe me not!' he yelped, excitedly. 'No cargo work today, it's some kind of holiday and the Chinese dockers are challenging us to a game of football. They are *challenging* us! Evidently there's a football pitch behind the old Seamen's Club.'

We'd never heard of anyone having a day off in China. And any dockers we had ever seen in the past nine months stood five-foot nothing and were bow-legged. The prospect of having a game of football with them was ludicrous. But it was also a terrific break from our nightmare of round-the-clock hard graft.

The Seamen's Club was a relic from years gone by, a two storey wooden building that sold little of value except Tientsin beer and Chung-Hwa cigarettes. Some of us had heard about the derelict football pitch behind the club but the grass and undergrowth, we were told, stood at least two-foot high in places.

Those in authority expected us to be there at two o'clock. It was a three-mile hike to get to the club and that didn't give us much time to get suitably dressed for the event. As usual in those circumstances, old uniform shorts, shirts and socks were dug out and those that had none, used working clothes. Engine room shoes or working boots were bound to our feet with tape or string before we set out on the three-mile hike, followed by our loyal supporters, the entire Hong Kong Chinese crew.

The roar of the crowd was heard long before we reached the football ground. We looked at each other in dismay. As we approached the field of battle, the crowd parted to allow us to walk on to it. They laughed and hooted and pointed at us in our funny gear. It was all one terrific joke to them, a pantomime of sorts and we were the clowns.

School children were everywhere, whole battalions of them in bright red school caps and neckerchiefs and each one carrying a red flag. This was to be a special day for them. To them, we were the Christians about to be fed to the lions and they loved it.

The grass on the pitch had been cut so short it looked like a snooker table, all the lines carefully marked out and a flag fluttered at each corner. Behind each flag a man in a Communist Party uniform stood with a drum. Makeshift terracing had been built to ensure every spectator had a good view of the field and where there was no terracing, trucks, buses and vans were put to use as platforms.

'Not quite what we expected, Bob.' The Captain looked around at all the pointing fingers and the sea of jeering faces.

I called to our junior third Engineer. 'Mai Mo, let's kick the ball around.'

Some time was spent passing the ball to each other when suddenly a terrific roar went up and the opposing team appeared. They came out of their bus and trotted round the perimeter of the field, waving to the crowd, while we stood and gaped at them in disbelief.

Each member of the opposing team stood six foot tall and had muscles. They had trotted round the perimeter of the field, waving to the crowds and not one of them was breathing hard when they'd completed the circuit. Had we made that run with them it would have taken us four hours to recover.

They were immaculately dressed in red shirts, shorts and stockings and their football boots were brand new. They preened themselves before us. Their captain pointed at Davy, our centre-forward, and said something in Chinese that made his team laugh.

The Captain and I looked at each other, feeling we had already lost, feeling we should all quietly turn round, put our tails between our legs and go back to the ship.

Davy trotted up to us. 'We're in with a shout!'

We looked at him in amazement. 'You mean to play against this lot? Davy, you're a nut case!'

The others gathered round us and Davy went on. 'They're athletes, but they are not footballers. All their kit is new, brand new, stuff that they've never worn before, so they might be bigger than us and fitter than us, but *can they play football?*'

His words put a different slant on everything. Suddenly there was a glimmer of hope on our horizon and the game began.

After fifteen minutes we showered blessings upon him when he and our two Hong Kong schoolboy champions broke through the Chinese defence and slammed home the first goal. The crowd was silent and we felt we were not too popular.

Our second goal was a little more difficult when the referee gave the other side a foul every time one of their players and ours bumped into each other. But when they slammed into us with boots flying, nothing was done about it. From my position as right back, I managed to stay clear of most of the shoulder charges, kicks and violent pushes. When the ball came my way I lobbed it up to our front line. The game was becoming more violent. Even so, Davy again smacked the ball past their goalkeeper. We were literally a three-man team but our men were tiring.

The crowd was beginning to thin out a little. We saw school children being herded off and there were no longer any drummers at the corner flags.

We seemed to have gained our second wind and being two goals up against such odds inspired us tremendously. The two schoolboy champions attacked the opposition's goal line repeatedly and the more they were manhandled or penalised, the more they fought to get through. Their determination inspired the others.

Evidently our hosts didn't know about 'half time' or had chosen to ignore it, so the play continued, with a difference. They turned nasty and we didn't retaliate. They didn't go for the ball, they went for the legs of the player and our side were accumulating lots of cuts and bruises.

Suddenly little Mai Mo collected a loose ball, made his own way through and cracked in goal number three.

The cheers of our twenty-plus supporters were clearly heard in the silence that now filled the whole area, an area that had earlier been filled with the shouting of thousands of excited schoolchildren.

They had disappeared. No little schoolchildren with flags and no spectators perched on top of buses or vans. Little groups of men stood sullenly behind the home team's goalposts and the men from our ship danced and jumped about behind ours.

Our opponents centred the ball but the heart had gone out of them. They had come to humiliate us and instead, they were the ones who had failed. Ten minutes later, our two Hong Kong schoolboy champions belted in goal number four.

Scoring goals was now quite easy!

Davy was now limping badly and could no longer run with the ball. Most of us limped when we moved, but pains were ignored when we went after a ball.

They literally stopped playing after our fifth goal and with half an hour's time left, the home team picked up their ball and made their way off the pitch to where their bus was waiting. Their referee was furious, stamping his foot and shouting his head off while his whole team shuffled along and suffered his abuse without saying a word.

I stood and looked at our team. They didn't know what to do or say. We were battered and bruised about the legs but that was of little consequence at that moment. It was a strange victory. Mai Mo, Hui Ying, Kwan Cheung and Lok Po Mai had played brilliantly and were bewildered by their success now it was over. They gathered into one group and our supporting crew members ran on to the field, cheering and dancing round them.

Davy, slowly and painfully limped all the way across the pitch and up the slope to the bus where the Chinese team had gathered. He contemptuously pushed their referee to one side in the middle of his tirade then walked over to the captain of their team and put out his hand. He stood like that, without moving.

Their captain hesitated, a thousand thoughts coursing through his mind, muddled with what had been hammered into his head since childhood, what his authorities might do and what he'd just seen today. He looked at the outstretched hand.

A moment passed, then he solemnly shook hands with Davy. Another player moved forward and shook Davy's hand. From where we were standing we saw this whole team solemnly take their turn in shaking his hand.

Somehow I doubt if Davy Stewart, from 22 Thomas Muir Street, Greenock, Scotland, ever tells anyone about the time he played in an International: The 'MV Inchmull' versus The People's Republic of Communist China and he had been the star of the show.

Or if Mai Mo, Hui Ying, Kwan Cheung, Lok Po Mai or the others ever tell their grandchildren about that day in 1958? I hope they do. Oh! Yes, I hope they do.

THE PIRATES

Our new Sparks had joined our ship a couple of weeks earlier and we were still pumping him for news of home. We were bored with lying at an anchorage in the Singapore Roads, waiting to go in.

'There was a big article in the Telegraph about pirates. A lot of talk and nothing else,' he informed us.

Old Bob Graham, the Chief Engineer was a man who always liked to get the facts right. He removed his pipe from his mouth and looked over the top of his spectacles at Sparks. 'I presume you mean the Merchant Navy Telegraph?'

'Yes, Chief. The latest was a Hamburg Line job. Evidently they all obeyed the Master Mariner's Code of Conduct, which says – 'offer no resistance, let the pirates take what they want.' And they took everything they wanted. A big load of nothing. Watches, clocks, radios – anything they considered of value. The rule book is rubbish. These blasted pirates could have chopped everybody's heads off, tossed us to the sharks and nothing would have been done about it.'

Dougie the Mate snorted, 'I'd have had a go at them. I'd have made them think twice.'

Paddy Keilly, our Second Mate and I looked at each other and said nothing. We knew the Mate was, as the Irish would say, 'all mouth and no trousers'.

So we were lying at anchor outside the main waterway into Singapore and the heat was slightly excruciating. The smoke room's overhead punka fan was slowly pushing the hot air around and every porthole and door was wide open. All six of us sat, dressed in white uniform shorts, towels round our shoulders to absorb our sweat, a pair of flip-flop sandals and nothing else. Our lungs moved in and out but they didn't seem to pump much air. Cold beer had a cooling effect and was necessary to replenish the sweat trickling down our bodies.

Our ship's complement consisted of six British officers, six Chinese officers and twenty- two Chinese crew members, ranging from a Bosun on deck, a Number One Donkeyman in the engine room, then down a long, long way to an officers' pantry boy called 'Unga'.

Unga's whole name was written 'Ng', but how does any normal person pronounce 'Ng'? So, to us, he was 'Unga'. Evidently, in his part of China, if a baby's mother died in childbirth, the baby was rejected as bad luck by all members of the family and wasn't officially given a name. Usually it was referred to with a grunt and palmed off to beggars or thrown into a river to drown. So Unga had no knowledge of a family or a childhood, except for the vaguest recollections of sailing and working with strangers in junks and sampans.

This start in life led him to adulthood with a skeletal body of average height, few teeth and an enormous smile that showed what few teeth he had. No one ever knew where Unga slept. He could be found ironing bed linen at two in the morning and yet happily interrupting his work to run and make anyone a cup of tea. In a competition for good looks he could easily win the title of being the ugliest Chinaman in the whole of the People's Republic of Communist China and its neighbouring countries and the verdict would be unanimous.

I was Wee Bob, the Second Engineer, though at five-foot-six inches I think the title was due to my tender years in those far-off days as much as to my stature.

Captain Mel Hooper and Chief Engineer Bob Graham were pipe smokers. When we were at anchor on evenings like this, their smoke hung in the atmosphere and was only slightly disturbed by the overhead punka fan.

'Sho'eside people come ship.'

The call came from the Chinese quartermaster on gangway duty that was now standing in the smoke room doorway with a huge smile on his face. He then briskly stepped aside to allow the 'sho'eside' people to enter.

The 'sho'eside people' consisted of a frail, old man in tropical whites supported by two very attractive ladies. Four more beautiful members of the opposite sex followed, gorgeous creatures that could have graced the centrefold pages of 'Playboy' magazine. There didn't seem to be any more.

I vacated my chair with alacrity and the two ladies gently eased the old man into it. The Captain and the Chief rose but the others remained sitting as if stunned before scampering off to don shirts.

The old man looked round all of us for a moment then wheezed. 'I'm John Smith, captain, master mariner, owner and general dogsbody of the yacht now moored alongside your ship. We are low on fuel oil, provisions, some spirits and, may I add, gentlemen, a cold beer would be greatly appreciated.'

'Unga!'

But our super-efficient Unga was already there with a tray of cold beers and glasses. One of the girls assisted him to pass the refreshments round, then, taking his arm, escorted him back to his pantry.

Another one of the girls sidled up close to me. 'My name is Gail. What's yours?'

The question took me quite by surprise and it took me a few moments before I could remember it off hand, then I blurted out. 'Bob. I'm Second Engineer.'

'Ah, Second Engineer Officer. You wouldn't happen to have about forty gallon of diesel fuel stowed away somewhere would you?'

Her lovely eyes were smouldering in her beautiful face and her perfume was making my heart shout 'WHOOPEE'!

'Diesel fuel? Diesel fuel?' I struggled to gather my wits. 'Yes, no problem. Forty gallons? Diesel fuel?'

She nodded. Her big blue eyes were playing havoc with my senses. Her perfume was making my knees shake and her breath was warm on my face.

'Just a minute. We have two hundred tons of diesel fuel on board. What kind of engine do you have?'

'Sixty horse power, turbo-blown four-stroke Berguis.'

I stammered. 'I've a forty gallon drum of gas oil, specific gravity about point eight four. It's purer than Diesel and we'll never use it on board this ship.'

She looked at me as if I'd offered her forty gallons of Chanel Number Five.

'Point eight four? Gas oil? Wow! Bob, darling, that's liquid gold!'

So hand-in-hand, shoulders touching, we strolled down aft together to the crew's quarters. Once there, I called out a couple of donkeymen to lower the forty-gallon drum of fuel oil down on to the deck of the yacht.

Meanwhile Unga was frantically lowering baskets of frozen chickens, meat, vegetables and frozen fish down on to the same yacht. Then I saw the two old seadogs, Captain Mel Hooper and Chief Engineer Bob Graham carefully lower a case of assorted spirits from the upperdeck down to the foredeck of the yacht.

The ladies were so beautiful, so friendly and we hadn't seen any beautiful ladies in a long, long time. We hadn't seen any ladies in a long, long time.

Yes, it was lovely, but soon it was over. We stood on deck and waved them off until their yacht eventually disappeared round the point at Achai Sound. Sadly, we returned to our smoke room. The perfume of those beautiful creatures hung in the still air. Nobody smoked.

Suddenly the Chief looked at Sparks. 'What did you say about pirates?'

This made us laugh.

'I gave them that drum of gas oil we couldn't use, Chief.'

'Good.'

'And she knew what specific gravities were.'

'I'm not surprised, Bob. She had a B.Sc. in thermodynamics. A Bachelor of Science with honours, actually.' He sighed and started to fill his pipe. 'The Captain and I had a long talk with the old man and the two girls that stayed behind with him.'

The Captain took out his pipe and lit it. 'It seems the old chap was in banking or something and got caught in an earthquake in the Philippines. He was crushed under a pile of bricks when a building fell on him. Rescuers heard the old man crying but it was thirty-six hours before they managed to dig him out. Cherry and Vicky were the two medical consultants who managed to put all his broken bones back together again. When he his bones were finally in some sort of working order he sold up everything, bought the yacht and had the girls join him. That was over three years ago.'

The Chief smiled. 'Sometimes they have to put him to sleep with a touch of chloroform or something. Or they sedate him with whisky, rum, aspirins and paracetamol. In fact anything that kills pain. Poor old fellow.'

The Captain pointed his empty pipe at us. 'All his crew are handpicked. No men. He's the only man on board. But do you know the bit that really got through to me? When he's in pain, one of the girls slips into bed with him and cradles him in her arms. No sex, nothing like that. Just cradles him like a mother would comfort a crying baby. Cradle him until the crying stops and he goes back to sleep.'

We all pondered on this. It was difficult to imagine the dream, or the reality, of a yacht with a crew of six beautiful young ladies, each one highly qualified in her own particular field.

We sat in silence.

Finally, the Mate cleared his throat. 'Where's Unga? He usually has the empties cleared away by now and brings in the beers. Hell! Where is he? UNGA!' he roared.

One of the Chinese stewards came in and started to clear away the empty bottles.

'You like mo' beer?'

'Yes. Six more beers. Where's Unga?'

'In pantly.' The steward stood, wringing his hands and looking worried. 'Not good. Maybe, I think you come look-see?'

The fact that for the first time ever, Unga was not scurrying around attending to our every wish puzzled us. We looked at each other then rushed to the pantry to find him sitting on his little stool, gazing into the far distance with unseeing eyes, completely oblivious to the presence of the six officers that crashed into his little pantry and stared at him.

I turned to the Chinese assistant steward.

'What's wrong with him?' I whispered.

He looked at me and smiled. 'Me not know. Cook not know.' he sighed, then shook his head sadly and his lower lip trembled. 'We all think maybe one shoreside lady give Unga a big kiss.'

THE JONAH SHIP

The years had caught up with me and my high blood pressure was at record levels. A spell in the Dreadnought Seafarers Hospital did work a few miracles but not enough and my days spent deep sea were finally over.

She was my first coaster and Ivar had bought her. This bold Ivar stood well over six feet tall and was as round as he was tall. He was a Swede by birth, proud owner of three coasters and convinced that this latest acquisition to his fleet was to be his flagship. Whispers that she was a Jonah ship did not deter him even slightly, for Ivar was not the superstitious type. Not until later, that is.

He bought her and renamed her M.V. 'Roti'. A measure of economy was achieved by chiselling off the end letters of her original name 'Barotia'.

She was the fifth of six ships of that design and where the other five performed very sweetly, the 'Roti' was cursed.

Apparently the Barotia's evil ways had rapidly bankrupted her first owner, a Greek merchant, and this forced him to abandon his crew of Greek seamen and leave them stranded and unpaid in the port of Ayr in Scotland. After a month's misery the crew retaliated by setting fire to the ship's accommodation to draw attention to their plight. This resulted in the Greek authorities being obliged to intervene and fly the Greek seamen home.

Further pressure on the Greek authorities resulted in some local semi-skilled handymen being employed in making enough repairs in the hope that she may, one day, be sold.

When I joined as Chief, the stench of smoke still hung in the atmosphere and there were damp patches and little puddles everywhere, compliments of the firemen's hoses. The wooden panels above my head faintly displayed the words 'Lipton's Tea' and the rug on my cabin floor faintly bore the title 'Regent Flour Mills.' Layers of white undercoat paint nearly covered most surfaces and new electric wires in the alleyways were entwined with the old ones.

Some articles were new, though of poor quality. All linen had been replaced, the bunk had a new mattress but my chair looked like a reject from the backyard of a local pawn shop. I could honestly say that the accommodation on board this coaster was quite different from what one would expect to find on a modern cargo ship.

There were a few touches of sabotage in the engine room to rectify before the main engine, the generators or auxiliaries could be induced to function in any way. Nothing was straightforward, many parts had been tampered with and we had to be off the berth at 6am. I finally staggered into my bunk and had one hour's sleep before we sailed.

The main engine settled down, the Volvo diesel generator battered away merrily on full load, the starting air bottle was topped up and the De Laval oil purifier was rattling ominously but filling the daily service fuel tanks nevertheless.

Smoking diesel engines, multiple fuel leaks and water dribbling down where water should not have been dribbling down were faults that I chose to ignore temporarily. I just needed to sit down for a while to rest my aching bones.

'Hey, Sheef, I come to give you help, yes.'

'Hold it, Ivar, everything is OK. Let her settle down...'

But he never gave me a chance to finish. He wanted to play with his new toy. 'Engine better on fresh water cooling. Sea water cooling no good. I show you this thing.'

He immediately started to open and close assorted valves in the main engine and diesel generator cooling systems, but it was obvious he didn't know what he was doing. He hadn't a clue what he was doing. All the water in the fresh water header tank went overboard, the sea water valves were now shut and the main engine and generator were covered in a blue haze. The alarm sirens were screaming hysterically and this added to the pantomime.

I stopped the main engine, threw open some valves and managed to push some sea water through its cooling system before anything seized, cracked or blew up.

'What for you do this thing, eh? This one my ship, eh?'

So we had lots of words, most of them four-lettered, all of them loud and we came very close to walloping each other. Eventually, he stormed off after agreeing to leave the running of the engines to me.

On the voyage from Ayr to a little known port upriver from Hull I was rapidly finding many more little mementos left by the former engine room staff. Sweet little tokens gifted by my predecessors, like pipes that were plugged with rags, valves with their insides removed and engine crankcase doors slackened off so copious amounts of lubricating oil leaked into the engine room bilges.

My first early morning start ended when I flopped into my bunk twenty-six hours later.

Then there were my fellow crew members. The Mate was a Bulgarian. He was banned from Bulgaria and its surrounding countries although I never found out why he was banned from anything. He always looked half asleep when he moved. Neither did he sit with us at the mess room table at mealtimes. Instead, he opened the door of the pantry refrigerator and ate pieces of anything within a hand's reach until satisfied. When he had eaten his fill he would carefully close the refrigerator door, wipe his hands on the front of his uniform jacket and wander off. Finding a ham shank with bites out of it or a bowl of custard with a few handfuls scooped out were common events. Ivar told me he lived in France but I found he couldn't speak a word of French.

So I had an Ivar whose surname I didn't know and a mate whom we just referred to as 'the mate.'

The remainder of the 'Roti's' merry band were two Cape Verde Islanders, Manuel and Tony.

Manuel was a hyperactive knife man with some knowledge of English and Tony was his shadow.

I spent many long hours in the engine room and achieved quite a lot, so had little contact with either of them. Manuel was an idiot by anyone's reckoning but he was an idiot with a big knife, so I didn't tell him I knew he was an idiot.

Ivar was not the brightest of men, either. I staggered out of the engine room for a cup of coffee one day and met him coming out of the galley.

'Ah, Sheef, we arrive Colstis Portby maybe seven o'clock time. OK?'

'Ivar, is that seven o'clock tonight or seven o'clock tomorrow morning?'

'Yes,' he replied cheerfully and continued on his way. As I said, communicating could be difficult.

Our two Cape Verde Islanders, Manuel and Tony would disappear ashore in every port we stopped at round the coast and when they returned they were usually accompanied by a couple of hard-faced whores or a horde of outraged policemen.

When we arrived in one port upriver from Hull, four such policemen came on board, handcuffed our two worthies and took them ashore for reasons that were never disclosed to anyone except Ivar. The knife went too.

Within the hour we had an English bosun and a seventeen-year-old boy who looked thoughtful and chewed gum very slowly.

Until that day I was fortunate enough to stay one jump ahead of the Jonah ship's evil ways if one discounts the hours I slaved. But she caught me viciously as we sailed down the Humber on our way to Rotterdam.

The Volvo diesel generator suddenly overheated without warning and a pipe connection burst as I reached to shut it down. Live steam roared up the left sleeve of my boiler suit, scalding me from the tip of my little finger to my armpit.

Now one-handed with my teeth clenched, I started the two small Ford generators, put them on load and phoned Ivar on the bridge to tell him of this latest inconvenience but emphasised that we could continue to Rotterdam.

The pain was starting to get really bad now, so I came up out of the engine room and went to my cabin.

The new English bosun and the boy appeared minutes later and found me trying to ease myself out of my boiler suit.

'Just a minute, Chief, let's do it my way.'

He produced a large pair of scissors and started cutting my boiler suit open from my wrist to my neck.

'What's your name, bosun?' I asked the question through tightly clenched teeth.

'Neil Reid.'

'What's the boy's name?'

He was standing next to us, still chewing and watching everything that was going on. In his hands he held a large jar labelled 'Petroleum Jelly, for industrial use only.'

Neil stopped cutting and turned to look at him. 'What's your name?'

The face stopped chewing and he looked at each of us in turn.

'Why?'

Neil's scissors shot to within a few millimetres of the boy's left nostril.

The boy answered softly. 'Denys. D-e-n-y-s.'

Neil then returned to cutting open the sleeve and side of my boiler suit. Eventually it was opened up enough to expose the mess that was once the underside of my left arm. The boiler suit dropped to the floor and I stepped out of it. The skin hung in shrivelled drapes and the whole arm looked as if it was wrapped in a cloth of Royal Stewart tartan.

Neil looked it over for a moment. 'Stay there, Chief, I'll be right back.'

He left me standing in my underpants, vest and engine room socks. I was in agony now my burnt arm was exposed to the air.

'Well, Denys with a 'Y', have you ever seen anything like this before?'

He stopped chewing while he surveyed the mess. Then he looked at me and drawled, 'My father got burnt last year.'

'Was it serious?'

'Yeah. Well, they don't muck around much in them crematoriums, Chief.'

He might have been trying to be funny but I don't think I was in a laughing mood.

Neil returned at that moment with one of the ship's new tablecloths and the moment passed. He gently smeared my whole arm with the Petroleum Jelly, wrapped it in a large square cut from the tablecloth and bound it with plastic tape. I sat down on the day bed, he covered me with my blanket, then he and Denys left.

The Roti clattered all the way to Rotterdam and I felt the bitch was happy she had included me among her victims. Sometimes she would roll a little to add to my discomfort, but even so, the long hours I'd spent in the engine room caught up with me and I slept.

On arrival at the busiest port in all Europe, the 'Roti' was invaded by Customs and Excise, Immigration, the Shipping Agent, a Harbour Pilot and staff, the Padre from the Missions to Seamen and a doctor to confirm that there was no plague, diseases or undesirables on board.

Their cars were parked on the dockside and we were abandoned at the seaward end of a long narrow jetty. There were sounds of movement outside my door and lots of people talking and shouting at the same time.

A pompous little twit suddenly stepped into my cabin without bothering to knock.

'Are you the Chief Engineer who needs a doctor?'

He probably came to this conclusion by seeing the brass plate on the door that said 'Chief Engineer' and the fact I was now sitting half-naked with my left arm wrapped in a tablecloth.

I confessed to being the Chief Engineer and, yes, I needed a doctor. I may have been a little abrupt in my response but I had lost a lot of sleep in the last forty-something hours and the pain in my arm was still slightly more than just excruciating.

'I am from the Shipping Office. We have sent for a doctor to attend to your arm. He will be here soon,' he said haughtily and turned to leave.

'Just a minute!'

He turned back and raised his nose a few centimetres higher.

'Yes?'

'I want a taxi in a couple of hours from now to take me to North Sea Ferries Terminal.'

He glared at me then groaned silently and scribbled something in his notebook.

'Will that be all?'

'And I want a ticket to Hull.'

Again he glared at me for a full sixty seconds before filling out a form in his pad. He scrawled his signature on it, slapped it on my desk and left before I had any more requests. I don't think he liked me very much.

The doctor came next. He cut away my piece of tablecloth, took his scissors and cut off the shreds of skin that dangled from my little finger to my armpit, then washed off the Industrial Petroleum Jelly. When he picked up a dark brown bottle out of his bag I noticed that the word 'Iodine' is nearly the same in Dutch as it is in English. So he washed the raw flesh in my arm in Iodine, wrapped it in pads and bandages and left without a word. That pained me.

Time passed. I was attired in an old pair of slacks, a vest, underpants, and socks and I needed a shower badly. I undressed slowly and carefully. With my left arm sticking out at right angles from my body I spent some time trying to tie a bath towel round my waist. I failed, my patience left me, so I walked to the shower with the towel held in front of me, then showered and staggered back to my cabin, soaking wet.

I was met by Neil Reid and a very large Scotch. 'You poor bastard', he said softly. Then he dried me off and dressed me, ready to go ashore.

He was packing my suitcase when our Bulgarian mate entered the cabin.

'The Captain, he want for you up top. Cargo start very quick soon.'

Neil put a hand on his chest, ejected him backwards out of the cabin, shut the door and returned to packing my gear. Finally, he stuffed all my official papers, my wallet and my free ticket on North Sea Ferries into my pockets.

'Your taxi should be at the end of the jetty by now. Just tell the driver 'North Sea Ferries' and even if the bugger doesn't speak English, he'll understand that.'

So Neil saw me off the 'Roti' and on to the jetty where we shook hands. I walked along with my suitcase in my right hand, sick of the pain in my left arm and sick of being so weak and useless.

'Hey, Sheef!'

I turned and saw Ivar on the wing of the bridge, waving. 'When your arm is fixed good, you come back. OK?'

I waved in return, picked up my suitcase again and carried on my long walk towards the dock area.

He was sitting in his car reading a newspaper when I arrived and dumped my suitcase on the back seat then gingerly edged in to the passenger seat beside him.

'Right, mister, North Sea Ferries.'

He looked at me puzzled and shook his head. He also waved his hands and blabbered at me in Dutch.

I repeated, 'North Sea Ferries'. This time I raised my voice.

He could see my bandaged arm and smell the stink of the iodine so he smiled at me sympathetically, shrugged his shoulders and took off.

Under my breath I found myself cursing, 'Hell and Damnation to big fat Swedes, Cape Verde Islanders with knives, bewildered Bulgarians and the Dutch, especially Shipping Agents and the Dutch pig of a doctor who washed my burning arm with iodine and stupid taxi drivers that wobble and bounce battered old Citroens along bumpy dockyard roads.'

At the terminal the driver drove right up to the entrance and helped me out of the car. While I fumbled for my wallet he made off with my suitcases and hurried to the ticket and luggage counter.

He was all smiles when he spoke rapidly in Dutch to the bright young thing behind the counter, then he backed away, still smiling and waving to me. He turned and hurried out the terminal doors.

'That taxi driver! He's off and I haven't paid the twit.'

The bright young thing giggled. 'He asked me to tell you, sir, he is not a taxi driver. He is just a local newsagent and he was waiting at the docks for a delivery of today's newspapers.'

Well, maybe the Dutch are not so bad after all. Maybe life on board coasters is not so bad either? I recall I sailed with Ivar four times and I never heard of any Chief who sailed with him more than once!

Hell, thinking back, age permitting, I might just like to do it again.

Bob Jackman

THE ORKNEY TRIP

A super tanker had blown sideways in a sudden squall and damaged the underwater pipeline at Flotta in the Orkneys. Repairs had been carried out but those in authority decided that the repaired pipe should be covered with gravel as an added protection.

Messages were sent out to find a hopper, and for those unfamiliar with contraptions that float and move on the surface of the sea, a hopper is a small ship with a bottom that can be opened hydraulically from the deck, thereby dropping its cargo on to the sea bed.

Eventually, after a flurry of telephone calls between shipping offices, an old hopper was located, abandoned on a deserted beach in the Moray Firth. A mass of assorted handymen were given the task of patching it up and overhauling enough of the engine room machinery to get her off the beach and capable of moving under her own power.

Their next requirement was a Chief Engineer and a Captain. However no sensible qualified personnel within five hundred miles in any direction would go near her when informed of the situation.

But there were two of us that did: One being a Captain Jack from Largs and the other my humble self, Chief Engineer Jackman from Scarborough.

The Captain was very much a Clydesider. He had the same stocky build as I have, but he was abrupt and talkative where I often thought twice before I spoke, then forgot what I was going to say. Age and indifference were the prices we had to contend with.

Our travel arrangements had been made by an agency in London that gave instructions for us to find our own way to a certain five star hotel in the heart of Edinburgh and from there we would be escorted to a plane that would take us to Invergordon. The fact that Merchant Navy personnel often had to find their own way to ships in remote corners of the world that could not be found with a magnifying glass in a detailed school atlas, was not accepted by the agency who organised this trip to Invergordon.

It was of very little consequence because the escort made no appearance.

The Captain snorted, 'I bet the twit got lost finding his way to Edinburgh.'

It would seem he had no love for agents.

Since all our expenses would be paid by the aforementioned London office in charge, we indulged in an excellent evening meal and indulged in a bottle of best Bordeaux. We ordered coffee and Drambuie liqueurs to follow.

A wine waiter floated to our table. 'Could I recommend this very rare old malt, gentlemen?' he purred. He correctly guessed we were Merchant Navy Senior Officers and Head Office somewhere in the South would be paying the bill. 'It was twenty years old when the hotel first stocked it and that was twenty years ago. Perhaps a sample, gentlemen?'

On our acceptance he poured two measures of rare Drumguish Cairngorm malt, then stood back and watched our faces.

'Leave the bottle.' We spoke simultaneously and a few measures passed before we replaced the cork.

Captain Jack swilled the remains of his malt around the bottom of his glass thoughtfully. 'The agents for this Oil Company in London made all the arrangements for you and me to come to this hotel where we would be met and escorted to a plane that would fly us to Invergordon. It is now nine o'clock and no escort has, as yet, arrived. So I suggest we take two rooms for the night, have a hearty breakfast and take a taxi to Invergordon in the morning.'

'How long would it take for a taxi to get to Invergordon?'

'From here? Edinburgh to Invergordon? About three hours at the most.'

'And a plane?'

'By my reckoning, probably take about six and a half hours. Considering time taken to get to the plane, take off, flying time, time taken from airport to ship. Yes, probably six hours or more.'

'We'll take a taxi.'

'Aye, Chief, we'll take a taxi.' He paused for a few moments then spoke quite seriously. 'Some of these agencies have battalions of clowns sitting on their backsides in offices in London that think Scotland lies on the left hand side of the North Pole somewhere. I guess they wouldn't know where the Orkneys are or who they belong to.' He shook his head and sighed. 'Would you believe that when one of the staff phoned me, she insisted I make sure my passport was not out of date?'

Next day, we arrived by taxi at Invergordon Shipping Office in time for lunch. The taxi was paid for by the spluttering Oil Company representative, the clown who should have met us in Edinburgh. After a few minutes of the rough side of Captain Jack's tongue, the Oil Company's representative backed off and slipped into a taxi to journey to Inverness to board the Shuttle Flight to London.

So the Captain and I visited our hopper that afternoon.

She was antiquated, modified, patched up and had gathered many layers of rust and seawater scale over the long months she had lain abandoned on the beach. Internally, she was a scrap yard. Evidently her crew of three had beached her, walked off and would have nothing more to do with her.

I visited the engine room and it was obvious that the main engine had been run recently by the streams of oil that had trickled down the engine casing and the smell of soot and smoke that assailed my nostrils.

A small diesel engine connected to a sea water pump, air compressor and a dynamo lay on the starboard side of the engine room but it was most likely that it had never been run since Churchill was a boy.

The forward end of the engine room was stacked with 12-volt car batteries, three rows of them across the width of the engine room and some of them were new. A tangled mass of electrical wiring was spread over, under and around the batteries before disappearing at various points under the engine room floor plates to parts unknown.

Two men in dungarees were dismantling a small general service bilge pump.

'Are ye the new Chief? You're gonna tak' this thing up to the Orkneys?'

I replied in the affirmative.

They looked at each other and shook their heads sadly. 'Weel, we wish ye the very best o' luck, Chief. You've got a lot of nerve. That's all we can say.'

'Is there anything wrong with the pump?' I asked.

'We're just going to fit a new impeller. When it gets here, that is.'

But the new impeller didn't arrive until four o'clock in the afternoon and the two men in dungarees went back to work and fitted it.

'You won't get a test run of the pump until the main engine is running. The dynamo on the engine keeps the batteries fully charged, Chief. And another thing. You'll find you're working with three different voltages.'

That was lunacy! What clown thought it up?

It was nearly seven o'clock when we left Invergordon and headed for the Orkney Islands. The hopper's wheelhouse was about three feet square and the only extra that had been added since the end of World War Two was an overhead radar screen the size of a postcard.

Steering was manual and rusted. This meant that whoever was steering the hopper needed the strength of a Sumo wrestler to keep her on her course. When the Captain's strength started to give out, I took over, but since there wasn't room for two in the wheelhouse I was literally carrying the Captain on my back to do the navigation.

We went up the coast, crossed the mighty Pentland Firth in darkness and turned up into the Orkneys.

'This is bliddy marvellous, Chief,' the Captain gritted into my left ear. 'About ninety islands, low lying and not even a tree anywhere. There's places where it's miles deep, other places where you could paddle between the islands in wellie boots. I'm looking for a light at Yocca point but I bet it's not even lit. They only light it if they know you are coming. And another thing, the German fleet was scuttled here in 1919 so there's always the chance we could run into a partially submerged German battleship.'

I still had his comforting words in mind when, an hour later, it started to rain. There was no moon, not a star in the sky and our pleasure knew no bounds when we found the wheelhouse roof leaked. It was the Captain's turn to steer so I squeezed out of the wheelhouse and stretched my aching body.

A cast iron stove, oil fired, was fitted in the corner. We had been informed that when the hopper's bow dipped, the flame flared up dangerously. When the hopper's bow surged up, the flame went out.

'ELECTRICITY IS GOING OFF, CHIEF! RADAR IS FADING!'

Lighting on board was rapidly getting less when my feet hit the engine room floor plates. I guessed that the dynamo on the main engine was no longer pumping out any electricity, but it was just a wild guess.

I turned to the small diesel with the dynamo, air compressor and seawater pump attached and grabbed the cranking handle. There was no decompression lever! I remembered seeing a heavy screwdriver beside the rows of batteries and I wedged it into the spring of the exhaust valve. Now I could get the diesel to turn. I cranked and cranked until it picked up speed and yanked the screwdriver out of the exhaust valve spring.

The diesel went 'clunk' but didn't start. I took a deep breath and solemnly breathed the opening lines of 'The Lord's Prayer'. The second time I cranked her furiously she went 'clunk-clunk-clunk' and roared into life. I didn't care what the seawater pump or the air compressor were doing but we had electricity again! Oh! The sweet, sweet clattering of that poor little neglected diesel was the sweetest sound I had heard in years. Engine room lights slowly went bright again.

Up to the wheelhouse and the radar screen was working beautifully but the Captain was trembling so much he could hardly steer the hopper.

'Chief,' he wheezed. 'Oh, Chief, that was like driving a bus down Sauchiehall Street with your eyes shut.'

We were still in shock when we arrived at the tiny berth in Flotta and tied up alongside. There was a single track road from the berth to an ultra-modern construction further round the coast that could have been a hotel. The first streaks of the dawn were in the heavens and the only sound was the gentle lapping of the waves between the hopper and the berth.

Suddenly a Land Rover came hurtling down the single track road with a young lad driving. He talked a lot but, talk or no talk, within an hour he had us breakfasted and ushered into a bedroom each where we were left to sleep.

In the afternoon the Captain saw those in authority about ship's business and I arranged to have the services of two highly-qualified electrical engineers from Inverness to untangle the hopper's electrical systems. They renewed every length of wire, all things electrical and thoroughly tested everything connected with the hoppers electrics. Eleven twelve-volt batteries were placed out on the fore deck.

'When you leave, Chief, give them a wee float test. Just drop them over the side. If any of them float, send us a postcard and tell us about it.'

Meanwhile I lovingly serviced the little diesel that saved us from disaster on the run up to Flotta then found another few dozen other jobs that required my attention.

The hotel at Flotta was built for the oil personnel necessary to manage and maintain the terminal. The catering staff and dining saloon were of the highest order; they had a well-stocked bar, a cinema, a huge telly in the lounge, two snooker tables and a surgery.

Outside the surgery a very attractive young lady ambushed me and introduced herself. She stood very close to me. We shook hands. She moved closer. Our faces were almost touching.

'Chief Engineer Officer Jackman? I am Doctor Zoe Hertengal,' she breathed. 'I have been requested to check your blood pressure periodically while you are here. Could you come to my surgery, say, eight o'clock this evening?'

Her breath was warm on my chin. Her perfume should have been made illegal. There was no one else around.

I looked at her, smiled, let go her hand, said 'No' and continued on my merry way to the bar.

Captain Jack and I were probably the only two males on the wrong side of fifty-five out of all the men on that island and she was the only female. But he and I were seamen, and Flotta was not the first port we had been to and knew the wiles of pretty ladies. She could wait.

The next day, we made our first run from Flotta to Burray to take on a cargo of gravel. Children on their way to school stood at the side of the road to cheer and wave to this old clapped-out hopper chugging along their coastline and we waved back to them.

At Burray, an old lorry was waiting on the jetty to pour its first load of gravel down a shute into our hopper. Then it drove off a few times for more gravel until we were quite full. It was a slow business but it fascinated the school children who came to watch at every opportunity and ask questions. When we were fully loaded, we made the round trip to Flotta and back for another load. Weeks went by pleasantly with evenings of snooker, movies and tales around pints in the bar.

'Last load Saturday morning, Chief.'

'Aye?'

'I was just thinking. We could take all the school kids along for our last trip to Flotta. Let them see what it was all about. Then back to Burray, drop the kids off and sail to Invergordon.'

'Aye, a great idea!' I was in full agreement with Captain Jack's suggestion but I knew a few points would have to be cleared by those in authority. 'I take it the management in Flotta agreed?'

'Didn't ask them.'

'Good. The children's parents agreed?'

'They thought it was a good idea.' He paused for a moment. 'There were others who thought it was a good idea.'

'Aye, Captain? Who would that be?'

'The catering staff here at Flotta.'

So it came to pass that we loaded our last cargo of gravel at Burray that Saturday morning, took on eleven school children and headed for Flotta. Parents on shore waved and cheered as we went by and the kids jumped up and down with excitement.

They were fascinated on how the hopper's hold opened up when we dumped the gravel and they all had a try at steering. Finally they had a look down the hell-hole of the engine room but it scared them. But then, there were times when that hell-hole of an engine room scared me too.

Alongside the berth four stewards with a Land Rover appeared and hurriedly loaded us with bottles of soft drinks, boxes of cakes, chocolate biscuits and sweets while another kept a watchful eye on any bureaucratic busy body that might come from the hotel to investigate. They also gave us plastic bags of balloons and a gadget for blowing them up so we momentarily left a trail of balloons to mark our journey between the two ports we had sailed between during our three weeks in Orkney.

At Burray, parents came down to the jetty to collect their children, everybody was excited, fathers and sons shook our hands, mothers and daughters kissed our cheeks and everyone had so much to say. When we left, they waved to us until we turned at the headland and sailed out of sight.

So that was Burray, that was Flotta and we were now on our way to Invergordon. Neither of us had much to say so I cleared up any of the stuff that was left behind just for something to do. Everything down below in the engine room was clattering away quite merrily due to the hours I had spent overhauling the works.

I made two mugs of coffee on the stove that now functioned quite satisfactorily and took one to the Captain. The steering was another item that I had bullied into submission.

'Maybe I should have had my blood pressure checked, being our last night. That doctor, Zoe Hertengal, was a real passionate wench and I think she wanted it.'

The Captain looked at me over the rim of his coffee mug and smiled. 'Chief, if you had gone to the surgery you might have been disappointed. Your beautiful doctor went home on Wednesday and her replacement is short, fat and eats Garlic.'

'She eats garlic?'

The smile widened. 'No, *he* eats garlic.'

It was worth a laugh but our trip to the Orkneys was now behind us. We docked, tied up, and it was over.

There was a bus from Invergordon direct to Glasgow with few stops on route and to save the bother of changing trains in Inverness, we took it.

Somehow, we had little to say to each other. He was no longer Captain Jack, he was now 'Bill' and I was now 'Bob', not Chief, just two ordinary, elderly men sitting side by side on a long distance bus.

When we arrived at the bus station at Killermont Street we walked together towards the city centre. Bill was heading for the railway station in St Enoch's Square for his train to Largs. I was heading for the Central Station for my train to York.

We stopped at the corner of Gordon Street and West Nile Street, looked at each other and shook hands very firmly, but saying nothing. Words would only have spoiled what was going through our minds.

I turned and headed for the Central Station and the train home.

THE KISHORN HIGHLANDER

"They need a Second Engineer on a tug, Mr Jackman, up in the top left hand corner of Scotland somewhere. They want to sail it over to Sweden and tow a barge....'

In those far-off days Clyde Marine Recruitment never let me down. Since high blood pressure meant I was medically unfit for foreign travel they could always find me positions on things that floated, coastwise.

The Kishorn Highlander's main purpose had been to act as a ferry to a redundant oil rig off the Scottish coast and the high echelons of maritime bureaucracy eventually had forgotten it existed. This meant a leisurely life for the men on board, a life where they only moved when it pleased them.

The tug itself sometimes performed surprisingly well considering its main engine was only one of two built and its twin was installed in a railway locomotive somewhere in Eastern Europe. This was one of the facts that tended to deter some engineers from offering their services.

The halcyon days for those on board ended when they were informed that the Highlander was now chartered to make runs from Sweden to Heligoland and they were to be employed for a possible six weeks or so, in towing a barge loaded with gravel to make a breakwater.

It seems this did not meet the resident Chief Engineer's approval. 'Take this auld bucket through the Pentland, across the North Sea tae Sweden then run up an' doon tae Heligoland? Towing a barge? This thing couldna tow an empty cardboard box. You lot are on yer own, I'm off.'

And, true to his word, he left.

His replacement was an incompetent, idiot who was born and bred a mere twenty miles from the berth. He jumped at the prospect of being Chief Engineer on the Highlander, so he was 'signed on.' Then those in authority discovered he had worked in a bus depot in Perth and his technical abilities amounted to tidying up after the mechanics, washing bus windows or using a vacuum cleaner.

After travelling from Scarborough to this barren top left hand corner of Bonnie Scotland, I arrived on board and found the Kishorn Highlander and all five of the crew members seated in the mess room. They consisted of the Captain, the Mate, Second Mate, the AB, and their newly installed Chief Engineer.

The mess room was the only place on board the tug where the crew could all sit down together. A settee of sorts, four chairs, a table, a cupboard for dishes, a carpet so worn and dirty there wasn't a hint of its original colour and litter everywhere. An unwashed soup plate was pressed into service as an ashtray.

Heads turned to look at me then returned to the conversation they were not having.

I did not intend to stand there all day and I dislike being ignored. If they wanted to play funny buggers, I could play funny buggers, too.

'Are you all being replaced? Are you the new crew?' I raised my eyebrows and asked politely. Then it was my turn to keep my mouth shut while they now had puzzled frowns on their faces and asked lots of questions of which I evaded answering. Basically, being Glaswegian was crime enough but to move and live in England was unforgivable in their eyes. The captain pushed his chair back with a clatter and went ashore to telephone their office.

I had, metaphorically speaking, put the cat among the pigeons. No longer did they ignore my presence. In fact, I was shown which cabin was mine, informed the times of meals and learned that it was always the mate's turn to be cook. They asked questions I avoided answering but it was a lot better than standing in the mess room doorway and being ignored. I learned a lot about them. I don't think they even liked each other and this lack of friendship is rare in the far north of Scotland.

The Captain was a bad tempered tyrant. He didn't speak to his underlings, he barked at them and immediately took offence at anything they said. Authority was his weapon and he wielded it constantly.

The engine room presented no problems whatsoever though the new Chief trembled and interfered a lot next day when we got under weigh and sailed for Sweden. The Pentland Firth was as calm as a baby's bath water and the North Sea hardly rippled at all.

In Sweden I received a letter from my dear wife Mary and one of the pages came from Sam, our good neighbour's son. Sam was an Oxford schoolboy who had been playing with a ball when it bounced over the hedge into our garden. Being well mannered in all matters he made his way to our front door and requested permission to retrieve it. He duly retrieved the ball, had a glass of orange juice while Mary had a cup of tea and a strong friendship sprung up between them.

When I came home from sea after a short trip, I met Sam for the first time. In those distant days my main interest was investing in Unit Trusts. I drew graphs of their performances and invested in those I thought would profit.

I taught my pal Sam everything I knew and gave him an imaginary £10,000 to invest, win or lose. The page he included in my Mary's letter began; 'My Fidelity Special Situations and Jupiter Far East have done great! My £10,000 is now £11,061! I've made £1,061 profit in seven weeks! My shares rocketed!'

At lunch on the Highlander, I let the others read Sam's letter and they were suddenly interested in unit trust investments – all, that is, except the Captain who scanned Sam's letter disdainfully and made no comment. He just looked bored and kept changing the subject when investments were mentioned but I was now on good terms with the others.

In Sweden, we found our barge complete with its crane bulldozer apparatus and our cargo of gravel was soon loaded. We made our first trip to Heligoland, discharged the gravel as required and returned for more gravel. In Sweden, a rather smooth character slinked on board with a suitcase and had a whispered conversation with our Captain. When he left, clinking sounds came from the suitcase and the Captain had a sly smile on his face, particularly when he looked in my direction.

A whole case of whisky came on board with the stores on our second trip to Heligoland and the same smooth character was on board in Sweden before we were finished tying up alongside the jetty. By the time I had shut down the engines, everyone knew of the Captain's shady business dealings. They also had his orders not to tell me about them so they did, as soon as his back was turned.

The barge had a weird type of crane fitted with caterpillar tracks that could lift the gravel and dump it into the sea at the desired spot. It was operated by a docker. Once the gravel was dumped, we moved alongside the pier and some of us nipped ashore to stretch our legs and have a beer. The van from the ship chandlers appeared with the usual stores and provisions that had been ordered beforehand by the Captain. This time, however, instead of the usual supply of sausages, eggs and chips, there were also three full cases of Bell's Whisky, two full cases of Gordon's Gin and one full case of Bacardi Rum.

There were those of us who went ashore to stretch our legs and have a beer, and there were those of us who stayed behind to load the top secret stores away from seeing eyes.

We left Heligoland on a quiet misty morning, sailed past the point we had deposited our cargo of gravel and headed out into the North Sea.

The mate came down from the bridge while the rest of us were finishing breakfast. 'Phone call from shore, Captain. They want us to pull into Denmark. Something about the crane bulldozer thing is overdue a service, or something like that. There should be a couple of fitters waiting on the dockside when we arrive.'

'Aye, OK.' He wiped the grease and egg yolk off his breakfast plate with a piece of bread and pushed it into his mouth. He chewed it for a few minutes then snorted. 'You think you know about investments, do you?' He looked at me and shook his head in disbelief. 'I'll show you what a good investment is. You're gonna see what a good investment is.' Then he left.

We arrived in Denmark as the dawn broke. Two mechanics climbed on board and without a word to anyone, made their way to the crane and started to work on it.

Then six men, partly uniformed, came on board and came face-to-face with the Captain.

'Captain, we are Customs officers. We want to check your ship.'

'Yes! Och, aye, you are very welcome. Come away into the mess room and I'll just get you a wee refreshment. OK?' But his voice shook a little.

He hurried to his cabin and returned with a bottle of Scotch. He then busied himself in the mess room cupboard to find seven glasses then poured a good measure into each glass.

'Aye. Your good health, gentlemen.'

'Close the door, Captain,' the Head Customs Officer smiled. 'How much alcohol do you have on board, Captain?'

'Well, I've got this bottle and I think the mate has one. Maybe the Chief has one, but that's all. Aw! I assure you we know the laws in this part of the world.'

We were standing in the galley. A space had been cut in the dividing bulkhead to install the fridge-freezer and every word spoken in the mess room could be heard by those standing silently in the galley.

The Customs Officer knew we were there and listening.

'Do you know anything about three cases of Bells Whisky, two cases of Gordons Gin and one case of Bacardi Rum? I assume you still have them on board the ship, Captain?' He spoke very clearly for our benefit.

The Captain didn't answer.

The Customs Officer talked about the crime of smuggling alcohol from one country to another and the punishments involved.

'This alcohol is on board, Captain. I wish to see it.'

There was a shuffling of feet and chairs as three of them came out of the mess room with the Captain leading. They moved down the alleyway then through the small hatch on deck to the steering flat.

I was on deck with the others.

The mate had been standing outside talking with two of the lesser customs men who had found the duty mess room too crowded.

He informed us quietly. 'The Captain is to be fined eleven hundred pounds in our money and every time we go into a port he has to declare the six cases of alcohol to the port authorities. If there is as much as one bottle missing, he gets jailed.'

The accommodation door opened and the customs men came out, led by our Captain, quivering with fury.

His eyes held mine as he spoke to the Customs Officer. 'OK, sir, you caught me out and I am sorry. I promise I'll never try that again. But you knew exactly what I had in whisky, gin and rum. You even knew what brands they were, how many bottles, so someone must have informed you.' He then moved to stand in front of me, our noses inches apart, and his eyes boring into mine. 'I will ask for nothing more, sir. Who informed you?'

The Customs man looked at the two of us and smiled pleasantly. 'No one informed me, Captain. When you left the mess room to get your bottle of whisky to treat us all to a drink, you were stupid enough to have left the sales slip for the alcohol lying on top of the cupboard in your duty mess. One of my men just picked it up: Three cases of whisky, two cases of gin and one case of rum. So, good day to you, Captain, have a nice day.'

It proves you have to be careful with investments. If you want to steal, you have to do it legally.

FINALE

`Parting is such sweet sorrow'
The gospel of Shakespearians,
But I make bold to differ,
And quote from my own experience.
For I now nurse a broken heart,
And please, dear friends, don't doubt it,
For the sea and I are now apart,
And there's damn all sweet about it.

GENTLEMEN I HAD THE PLEASURE TO SAIL WITH:-

Malcolm Dryden
Joe Cochran
Bob Pocock
Eric Heppenstall
George Law
Louis Dupre
Angus Muir
Gordon Thomson
Harry Francis
Hughie MacPhail
Geoffrey Dunbar
Johnnie Blake
Frank Finlay
Bertie Wilson
Bob Stewart
William Jack

Jim Weir
Bob Graham
Bill Williams
Ted Oddie
Willie Wise
Johnnie Quigue
Ian Wallace
Brian St John Early
Charles Lorrimer
Ian Wallace
Norman Clive Green
J.E.V. Hood
Derek Bosley
Bill Halewood
Mel Hooper
John Carmichael

K.P. O'Mahoney
Al Savage
Danny Dyce
Bill Court
Bill Underwood
'Muscles' Manson
Jim Gray
Bill Halewood
Dougie Clegg
Billie Budd
Harry Bottomley
Angus Muir
Jimmy Hill
Ian Beaton
R. Hartley
John Patrick Bernard
Aloysis Ignatious
Quintus McMahon
Higgins
And others..........

Printed in Great Britain
by Amazon.co.uk, Ltd.,
Marston Gate.